THE
BEST
FAMILY
VIDEOS

SECOND EDITION

THE
BEST
FAMILY
VIDEOS

SECOND EDITION

Quentin & Barbara SCHULTZE

Augsburg
MINNEAPOLIS

For Steve and Beth

THE BEST FAMILY VIDEOS
Second Edition

Copyright © 1995 by Quentin J. Schultze

ISSN 1076-3783

The paper used in this publication meets the minimum requirements of American National Standard for Information Sciences—Permanence of Paper for Printed Library Materials, ANSI Z329.48-1984. ∞™

Manufactured in the U.S.A.   AF 9-2812

99   98   97   96   95   1   2   3   4   5   6   7   8   9   10

CONTENTS

INTRODUCTION

Welcome to the second edition of THE BEST FAMILY VIDEOS! We're grateful for the overwhelmingly positive response from readers of the first edition. And we worked hard to make the guide even better:

- an entirely new section on children's video series
- over 100 new entries, including feature films and movie-length TV dramas
- more easy-to-find video movies
- a new size that's even handier to carry

As with the first edition, we searched for the "best" videos we could find. Of course, "best" is a subjective word. Based on the appreciative responses of people of all ages who used the first edition, we're convinced that most people agree on the best movies:

- movies that really do what they claim to do (e.g., make us cry or laugh)
- movies with a positive view of life and a critical view of evil
- movies that are well written, well directed, and well performed
- movies that affirm wisdom and morality
- movies that are relatively free of potentially offensive language and scenes

So sit back once again, read some of the entries in our guide, and show your family and friends some of the best videos!

HOW TO FIND THE MOVIES IN THIS GUIDE

The avalanche of video movies available today doesn't always make it easier to find the ones you want to see. Except for popular new releases, it's often difficult to locate particular videos.

So here are a few simple rules that will make your video shopping more pleasant:

RULE ONE: Call ahead to the video shop. One phone call will usually determine whether or not a store has a video in stock. Unless you want to browse, don't waste a lot of time hopping from one store to another for a particular video. Some of the better shops will even put a "hold" on the tape for you or get a copy from another store in the same chain.

RULE TWO: Shop at more than one video store. The truth is that no two shops have the same videos, not even stores in the same chain. Managers often have their own preferences—and why not?

RULE THREE: Check the local public or college libraries. We've discovered video gems in libraries. Too many video-movie buffs forget to check one of the best sources of high-quality movies.

RULE FOUR: Compare the weekly movies listing in your local TV guide with your tapes-to-rent. Most television guides include a separate, alphabetical listing of all movies on TV for the week.

RULE FIVE: Get to know a local video shop manager. Sometimes they will order tapes if you can make a good case for why the store should stock it. By all means, use this guide to help make the case! In fact, ask the store to carry THE BEST FAMILY VIDEOS as a way of helping to generate customers for these types of movies.

KEY TO THIS GUIDE

Date: This is usually the date of release of the original film or, in a few instances, the airing of the original TV broadcast. Since there are multiple versions of some movies, and even completely different films with the same title, be sure to check the date.

Time: This is the approximate running time of the video version of each movie, *excluding* previews and credits.

Rating: This is the official Motion Picture Association of America (MPAA) voluntary rating code. It includes *G* (general audiences, all ages permitted), *PG* (parental guidance suggested, some material may not be suitable for children), *PG-13* (parents strongly cautioned some material may be inappropriate for children under 13), *NR* (not rated). We did not include any *R*- or *NC-17*-rated movies in this guide. Generally speaking, we think our appropriate-age guidelines are more helpful than the MPAA ratings, which address overt content, not thematic material.

Grade: This is our evaluation of the overall quality of the movie ($A+$ is outstanding, A is superb, $A-$ is excellent, $B+$ is very good, and B is good).

TVM: This refers to a made-for-television movie.

Audience: (*school-age* is six and older, *adolescent* is ten- to fifteen-year-old, *teen* is thirteen- to nineteen-year-old). These are approximate guidelines. If your children are above- or below-average maturity for their ages, or if they are simply sensitive to film content, you should adjust your thinking accordingly. *Mature teens* refers to well-adjusted teenagers who are emotionally like normal adults.

Content:

—*adult situations* are actual events that depict adults doing things that normally only adults do or at least that only adults normally understand. These include sexual situations, deeply personal adult discussions, war battles, and intense portrayals of bigotry and racism. Even though the situations might be positively portrayed, they will probably have to be explained to younger viewers.

—*adult themes* are topics or issues addressed in the movie which are normally of concern primarily to adults. These include such topics as divorce, war, adultery, suicide, racism, substance abuse, and debilitating illness.

—*intense dramatic scenes* are deeply moving, highly emotional events. They likely elicit strong audience responses, such as fear, anger, and sorrow.

—*language* refers to potentially offensive language, such as obscenity and profanity. We did not include films that are loaded with such language, yet we realize that some movies make moderate use of it for the sake of realism.

—*very rough language* refers to the most offensive types of language. We included only a handful of such films in this guide, in each case because we felt that the characters and story justified minimal use of such language.

—*violence* is any kind of violent activity directed against people or physical objects. It includes such things as explosions, nongraphic shootings, and fights.

—*mild violence* is very minor, nongraphic violence which would likely upset only the most sensitive viewers, especially children or adults with emotional problems. For example, slapstick violence is included here as it is usually seen as unrealistic and silly.

—*graphic violence* is explicit violence directly affecting people, such as shootings, bombings, or stabbings. Again, we included only a few of these films, always when we felt the violence was necessary for realism.

—*nudity* refers to any nongraphic, nonerotic displays of the naked human torso. It includes naked children and naturalistic nudity in tribal cultures.

Topics: We've suggested some possible topics for every movie. These are included for two reasons: (1) to provide additional information about the thematic content of each movie, and (2) to help parents, teachers, youth workers, and others to locate films which might facilitate discussion about important aspects of life.

CONTEMPORARY VIDEOS

ADVENTURES OF THE GREAT MOUSE DETECTIVE

A young mouse hires the great Basil, a famous detective, to find her kidnapped father in this lively, animated film based on Eve Titus's book, *Basil of Baker Street*. In Sherlock Holmes style, the great mouse detective matches wits with the evil Professor Ratigan. While searching for Olivia's father, he uncovers a nefarious plot against the queen, but in the end all is well, as the solution is "elementary."

Clues to a great adventure!

1986 80m G A- Animated

Audience: all ages
Content: intense dramatic scenes for children
Director: John Musker
Lead Cast: (voices) Vincent Price, Barrie Ingham, Val Bettin
Topics: children, heroism

ADVENTURES OF HUCK FINN, THE

Young Huck escapes his abusive pappy and his clean-living caretakers, sailing adventurously down the Mississippi with runaway slave, Jim. Only a few of the incidents from Twain's novel are included, and the duo are romanticized for their free-living ways. This laundered version of the classic tale is fun and folly with a few dramatic moments.

Huck Finn "sivilized."

1993 115m PG B +

Audience: adolescents to adults
Content: violence
Director: Stephen Sommers
Lead Cast: Elijah Wood, Courtney B. Vance, Ron Perlman
Topics: adolescence, family, friendship, nature, work

ADVENTURES OF MILO AND OTIS, THE

A dog named Otis must rescue his adventurous friend—a cat named Milo—who is swept away in a rushing river. Once rescued from the river, they wander through one adventure after another to find their way home again. Moore's narration gives life to this well-made film. If adults can put aside their sophistication, they will enjoy it, too.

A delightful adventure.

1989 76m G Japanese (English narration) B+ Animated

Audience: all ages
Content: nothing objectionable
Director: Masanori Hata
Lead Cast: (narrator) Dudley Moore
Topics: friendship, heroism, nature

AGE OF INNOCENCE, THE

Young attorney Newland Archer's plans for his future, which include marriage to sweet and proper May Welland, are jeopardized when her scandalous cousin arrives. Set in the opulence of 1870s New York society, this film is a delight to the eyes (Oscar for Costume Design) and the sensibilities. Based on Edith Wharton's award-winning novel.

Guilty of excellence!

1993 120m PG A+

Audience: mature teens to adults
Content: adult themes, language
Director: Martin Scorsese
Lead Cast: Daniel Day-Lewis, Michelle Pfeiffer, Winona Ryder
Topics: ethics, friendship, marriage, romance

AGE OLD FRIENDS

Two elderly men in a home for the aged together cope with growing senility and loneliness. When one of them is invited to move in
with a daughter and son-in-law, their mutually beneficial relationship is put at risk. A poignant portrait of aging filled with humor
and grace. Based on Bob Larbey's play, *A Month of Sundays.*

Eightysomething!

1989 86m NR TVM A

Audience: school-age to adults
Content: language, adult themes
Director: Allan Kroeker
Lead Cast: Hume Cronyn, Vincent Gardenia
Topics: aging, children, death, family, friendship

ALADDIN

The handsome street rat, Aladdin, and his pet monkey save the
Sultan and Princess Jasmine from an evil vizier who threatens to
take over the kingdom and marry the princess. Aladdin's secret
weapon is a genie living in a magic lamp. Terrific music and un-
believable voices, especially by Robin Williams as the Genie. Too
frightening for some young children.

Disney magic!

1992 108m G A+ Animated

Audience: all ages
Content: intense dramatic scenes
Director: Ron Clements, John Musker
Lead Cast: (voices) Scott Weinger, Linda Larkin, Robin Williams
Topics: family, friendship, heroism, marriage, romance

ALAN AND NAOMI

An unlikely friendship develops between a fourteen-year-old New York Jewish boy and a withdrawn immigrant girl from France during WW II. Naomi had witnessed her father's murder by the Nazis and is unable to overcome the trauma. Alan is enlisted to gain Naomi's trust and reintroduce her to life. In spite of his desperate need to fit in with his teenage peers, Alan reluctantly accepts the challenge "once or twice in a lifetime" to do something that will make a difference.

A powerful story of compassion.

1992 95m PG B+

Audience: teens to adults
Content: violence, intense dramatic scenes
Director: Sterling VanWagenen
Lead Cast: Lucas Haas, Vanessa Zaoui, Michael Gross
Topics: adolescence, death, friendship, religion, war

ALL CREATURES GREAT AND SMALL

A British veterinarian, his family, and his colleagues try to readjust to life in rural England after WW II. Vet James has difficulty accepting his roles as father and husband. This made-for-television film was part of a BBC series aired on public TV in the U.S. A splendid tale about love and thankfulness.

Based on the popular books by James Herriot.

1986 94m NR TVM A-

Audience: adolescents to adults
Content: nothing objectionable
Director: Terence Dudley
Lead Cast: Christopher Timothy, Carol Drinkwater, Robert Hardy, Peter Davison
Topics: family, friendship, nature, parenting, work

AMADEUS

As a forgotten old man, the mediocre composer, Antonio Salieri, recounts his painful acquaintance with a spoiled, crude, young composer named Mozart. Mozart's astounding music is heard throughout the film. Abraham, as Salieri, is superb and far outshines the erratic acting of Hulce as Mozart. Lavish sets and costuming enhance this splendid film.

A fascinating epic.

1984 158m PG A-

Audience: teens to adults
Content: language, adult themes
Director: Milos Forman
Lead Cast: F. Murray Abraham, Tom Hulce, Elizabeth Berridge, Simon Callow
Topics: death, ethics, family, marriage, romance, work

AMAZING GRACE AND CHUCK

A Little League pitcher who lives near a nuclear arms facility decides to give up baseball until such weapons are eliminated. Pretty soon professional athletes join his sports boycott, creating significant financial and political problems. Meanwhile, the boy creates tension between himself and his father, as well as among his peers. Slightly whimsical and very unrealistic, but remarkably compelling.

An inspirational tale.

1987 115m PG B+

Audience: all ages
Content: language
Director: Mike Newell
Lead Cast: Joshua Zuehlke, Alex English, Jamie Lee Curtis
Topics: adolescence, ethics, family, friendship, heroism, parenting

AMAZING GRACE WITH BILL MOYERS

PBS's Bill Moyers tells how and why the popular hymn, "Amazing Grace," was written by an 18th-century Englishman—a slave-ship captain turned antislavery advocate. The documentary also looks at how various artists have performed the hymn: pop star Judy Collins, opera talent Jessye Norman, gospel singer Marion Williams, folk singer Jean Ritchie, The Boys' Choir of Harlem, and country artist Johnny Cash.

An amazing story!

1990 87m G A

Audience: all ages
Content: nothing objectionable
Director: Elena Mannes
Lead Cast: various singers
Topics: prejudice, religion

AMERICAN STORY, AN

Six heroes return from the war with the Nazis to fight their toughest battle for freedom in their small Texas town. Recognizing that political corruption has taken over, they form their own party to challenge the system. A touching story of sacrifice for "the right thing" in the face of opposition even from those they love.

Is this a great country, or what!

1992 97m PG TVM A-

Audience: teens to adults
Content: mild violence, intense dramatic scenes
Director: John Gray
Lead Cast: Brad Johnson, Kathleen Quinlan, Tom Sizemore, G. W. Bailey, Patricia Clarkson, Lisa Blount, David Labiosa
Topics: ethics, friendship, heroism, prejudice, war, work

AMERICAN TAIL, AN

A curious young mouse is separated from his family when they emigrate from Russia to America in the late 19th century. Stumbling into one misadventure after another, he eventually becomes a hero in this cute animated tale about freedom and belonging. A welcome bonus is the portrayal of sibling affection rather than rivalry, best seen in the touching song, "Somewhere Out There."

Love can find a way.

1986 80m G B+ Animated

Audience: all ages
Content: intense dramatic scenes
Director: Don Bluth
Lead Cast: (voices) Dom DeLuise, Christopher Plummer, Nehemiah Persoff
Topics: family, friendship, heroism

ANGELS IN THE OUTFIELD

When a young boy asks God to help his favorite baseball team to "win a little," he witnesses angels helping his California Angels. Soon the skeptical manager believes in the kid—if not the angels—and the players begin to act and feel like winners. This remake of the 1951 film is a bit uneven, but it still entertains and inspires.

Heaven meets Hollywood—there's a miracle!

1994 97m PG B+

Audience: school-age to adult
Content: language
Director: William Dent
Lead Cast: Danny Glover, Christopher Lloyd, Tony Danza, Milton Davis Jr., Brenda Fricker
Topics: family, friendship, religion, sports

ANNE OF AVONLEA

In this excellent sequel to the miniseries, *Anne of Green Gables*, the teenage Anne begins her professional career as a teacher in Avonlea and develops romantic interests. Once again, things are bittersweet for Anne, who finds that real life is often not in tune with her hopes and desires. Another title is *Anne of Green Gables: The Sequel*. Based on the works of Lucy Maud Montgomery.

Exceptional family fare!

1987 227m NR TVM A Canadian

Audience: all ages
Content: nothing objectionable
Director: Kevin Sullivan
Lead Cast: Megan Follows, Colleen Dewhurst, Frank Converse
Topics: family, romance, work

ANNE OF GREEN GABLES

A precocious adolescent girl is adopted by a crusty spinster and her emotionally starved brother in eastern Canada. The girl's presence challenges her "family" and the rest of the community to reconsider their strict and sometimes unloving ways. Excellent performances, terrific scenes of rural Canada, and smooth direction make this movie a sure classic. Also see *Anne of Avonlea*.

Adaptation of popular book by Lucy Maud Montgomery.

1985 197m NR A Canadian

Audience: all ages
Content: nothing objectionable
Director: Kevin Sullivan
Lead Cast: Megan Follows, Colleen Dewhurst, Richard Farnsworth
Topics: adolescence, family, friendship, religion

ASSAULT, THE

During WW II in occupied Holland, a twelve-year-old boy's parents are executed by the Nazis for a crime they did not commit. Disturbed by the memories and confused by ambiguities surrounding the event, the boy seeks to understand what happened as he matures, marries, and practices medicine over the next forty years. A riveting, unforgettable film about war and the human condition.

Best foreign-language film Oscar.

1986 122m PG A+ Dutch (dubbed)

Audience: mature adolescents to adults
Content: language, violence
Director: Fons Rademakers
Lead Cast: Derek de Lint, Marc van Uchelen, Monique van de Ven
Topics: aging, family, heroism, marriage, parenting, war

ATTIC, THE: THE HIDING OF ANNE FRANK

This is the true story of Miep Gies, the young Austrian woman who helped hide Anne Frank's family in Amsterdam during the Nazi occupation of WW II. Gies married a Dutch citizen during the occupation to avoid Nazi deportation. As conditions worsened, she decided to risk her own life to save almost a dozen Dutch Jews, including Frank. This film is superbly crafted and deeply inspiring—a meaningful tribute to all who hid Jews.

A superb drama!

1988 97m NR TVM A

Audience: adolescents to adults
Content: intense drama, adult themes
Director: John Erman
Lead Cast: Mary Steenburgen, Paul Scofield, Huub Stapel
Topics: adolescence, death, heroism, religion, war

AU REVOIR LES ENFANTS (GOOD-BYE, CHILDREN)

A twelve-year-old boy beginning to discover the adult world takes a giant step into harsh reality when his new friend at the Catholic boarding school in occupied France turns out to be different from the other boys. They learn to trust each other, but the world's problems will challenge their friendship. When they say good-bye, it is good-bye to childhood.

A poignant, autobiographical film.

1987 103m PG A- French (subtitled)

Audience: teens to adults
Content: language, adult themes
Director: Louis Malle
Lead Cast: Gaspard Manesse, Raphael Fejto
Topics: adolescence, death, friendship, religion, war

AVALON

Three generations of a Jewish family deal with the American dream in 20th-century Baltimore. Each generation is more prosperous and successful than the previous one, but each also becomes less Jewish and less family-oriented. At times the story is slow, but the marvelous characterizations and humorous anecdotes of writer-director Barry Levinson win the day.

On the importance of tradition.

1990 126m PG A

Audience: adolescents to adults
Content: mild language
Director: Barry Levinson
Lead Cast: Aidan Quinn, Elizabeth Perkins, Armin Mueller-Stahl
Topics: aging, family, marriage, parenting, religion, work

AWAKENINGS

An introverted research physician devises a controversial drug therapy that awakens a small group of catatonic patients. It is a film of joyous rebirth and heart-wrenching slumber. Based on the work of Oliver Sacks, a brilliant psychiatrist whose own life is deeply changed by the listless patients he brings back to "life."

A celebration of the gift of life.

1990 120m PG-13 A

Audience: teens to adults
Content: mild language, adult themes
Director: Penny Marshall
Lead Cast: Robin Williams, Robert De Niro, John Heard
Topics: disability, ethics, friendship, romance, work

BABETTE'S FEAST

Two humble spinsters who lead a small sect in Denmark take in a cultured French refugee, Babette, during the 19th century. Babette's loving devotion to her kind "mistresses" is challenged by an unexpected windfall. Instead of setting herself free, Babette decides to sacrifice her fortune for the good of the community by preparing a fabulous feast that symbolizes love and reconciliation.

Won an Oscar for best foreign film.

1987 102m G A + Danish (subtitled)

Audience: teens to adults
Content: nothing objectionable
Director: Gabriel Axel
Lead Cast: Stephane Audran, Bibi Andersson, Bodil Kjer
Topics: aging, religion, work

BACK HOME

Culture clashes occur when an adolescent girl returns home to England after waiting out the war in America. She doesn't seem to fit in anywhere, but finds acceptance from an elderly friend and an equally ostracized boy. A beautiful, sometimes sad, story of how tolerance and understanding can open the door to love.

Take it home.

1990 105m NR TVM A- British

Audience: adolescents to adults
Content: mild violence, language
Director: Piers Haggard
Lead Cast: Hayley Mills, Hayley Carr, Adam Stevenson, Brenda Bruce, Jean Anderson, Rupert Frazer
Topics: adolescence, death, family, friendship, war

BACK TO THE FUTURE

Eccentric "Doc" Brown invents a time machine that sends Marty, a 1980s teenager, back thirty years to come face-to-face with his parents as teenagers. In spite of Doc's warnings, Marty can't avoid getting involved in his parents' earlier lives and altering the course of history. A crazy flight of fancy that pairs the incredulous Fox with the incredible Lloyd for a hilarious adventure.

What a trip!

1985 116m PG A

Audience: school-age to adults
Content: language, mild violence, intense dramatic scenes
Director: Robert Zemeckis
Lead Cast: Michael J. Fox, Christopher Lloyd, Lea Thompson
Topics: adolescence, family, friendship

BACK TO THE FUTURE II

Marty and his techno-wizard mentor, Doc, are launched via the DeLorean time machine into the year 2015. When he and Doc return to 1985, they discover that the villain, Biff, has also time traveled. The two heroes go back to 1955 in order to undo all the wicked gains Biff has made by being able to predict the outcome of sports events.

Jules Verne gone electronic.

1989 107m PG A

Audience: school-age to adults
Content: language, mild violence, adult themes
Director: Robert Zemeckis
Lead Cast: Michael J. Fox, Christopher Lloyd, Lea Thompson
Topics: heroism, romance

BACK TO THE FUTURE III

In the last of the *Back to the Future* trilogy, Marty and Doc travel back to 1885 to stop a potential killing. It's an old-style western in a contemporary sci-fi package, with romance, heroism, a gunfight, and a fabulous runaway train sequence. Not as glitzy as the first two, but the most pleasing tale with the fewest gimmicks.

The best of *Back to the Future*.

1990 118m PG A+

Audience: school-age to adults
Content: language, intense dramatic scenes
Director: Robert Zemeckis
Lead Cast: Michael J. Fox, Christopher Lloyd, Mary Steenburgen
Topics: heroism, marriage, romance

BEAR, THE

In this remarkably realistic tale, an orphaned bear cub takes up with an enormous Kodiak bear which is being stalked by ruthless hunters. Viewers experience the adventure largely from the perspective of the cub, which is naively tangling with other creatures and the land. Based on the novel *The Grizzly King*.

Wonderful animal adventure!

1989 90m PG A French

Audience: adolescents to adults
Content: violence
Director: Jean-Jacques Annaud
Lead Cast: Jack Wallace, Tcheky Karyo, Andre Lacombe
Topic: nature

BEAUTY AND THE BEAST

The heroine takes her captive father's place in the Beast's castle in 18th-century France. She and the beast both overcome their hesitations and fall in love, but not before Beauty is nearly married off to an evil suitor. This Disney classic is marvelously animated with fantastic music.

Best picture Oscar nominee.

1991 78m G A+ Animated

Audience: all ages
Content: violence, intense dramatic scenes
Director: Gary Trousdale, Kirk Wise
Lead Cast: (voices) Angela Lansbury, Robby Benson, Paige O'Hara
Topics: heroism, romance

BEETHOVEN

A St. Bernard puppy "adopts" a family and changes their lives. The slobbery beast proves his worth by clumsily aiding each member of the family. The movie has some hilarious moments, but its enduring value is its celebration of family love and commitment.

Roll over, Beethoven!

1992 84m PG A-

Audience: all ages
Content: mild violence
Director: Brian Levant
Lead Cast: Charles Grodin, Bonnie Hunt, Dean Jones
Topics: children, family, parenting

BEETHOVEN'S 2ND

The big lovable St. Bernard succumbs to romance and the Newtons' lives are disrupted once again—this time by four little fur balls. The mother's mistress hates dogs, but wants the puppies for the profit they would bring. While Beethoven mopes over his lost love, romance blossoms for the teens of the family and is rekindled in the adults when the pressures of work are laid aside. A gentler, warmer film than the original.

Puppy love!

1993 89m PG B

Audience: school-age to adults
Content: mild violence
Director: Rod Daniel
Lead Cast: Beethoven, Charles Grodin, Nicholle Tom, Christopher Castile, Sarah Rose Karr, Bonnie Hunt, Debi Mazar
Topics: adolescence, family, friendship, romance, work

BENNY AND JOON

Benny, a dedicated blue-collar worker, has decided he can no longer care for his schizophrenic sister, Joon, when an eccentric houseguest upsets the routine. This is a marvelous story of love, acceptance, and respect, beautifully filmed and treated with tenderness and hilarity. Depp will amaze you, Masterson will move you, and Quinn will command your respect.

Warm and funny.

1993 100m PG A +

Audience: adolescents to adults
Content: language, mild violence, adult situations and themes
Director: Jeremiah Checkik
Lead Cast: Aidan Quinn, Mary Stuart Masterson, Johnny Depp
Topics: death, family, friendship, romance

BIG

An early adolescent boy gets his wish to be in the body of a thirty-year-old man in modern America. He moves to New York City and gets a job with a toy company, but soon finds that adult life is not everything he expected. This story wonderfully contrasts childhood and adulthood, and surprisingly embraces the value of youthful innocence.

Academy award nomination for Hanks.

1988 102m PG B +

Audience: adolescents to adults
Content: language, adult situations and themes
Director: Penny Marshall
Lead Cast: Tom Hanks, Elizabeth Perkins, John Heard
Topics: adolescence, family, romance

BIG BUSINESS

Two sets of female twins are mistakenly switched at birth. One mismatched pair ends up running a big corporation that threatens to eliminate jobs in a rural, Southern town in which the other pair lives. When the two pairs tangle at the Park Plaza, the film turns into a wildly farcical comedy of errors.

Big comedy!

1988 94m PG B+

Audience: adults
Content: language, adult situations
Director: Jim Abrahams
Lead Cast: Bette Midler, Lily Tomlin
Topics: romance, work

BLACK BEAUTY

This well-crafted film was wrongly promoted as a children's movie, when in fact it offers a fairly dark and deep view of the book by Anna Sewell. The stallion narrates his own moving life in 19th-century England, from the glorious early years on a beautiful country estate to the gloomy days of an urban workhorse. Superb cinematography and a moving score.

An equine parable of life.

1994 87m PG B+

Audience: teens to adults
Content: violence, intense dramatic scenes
Director: Caroline Thompson
Lead Cast: Peter Davison, David Thewlis, Sean Bean, Jim Carter, Andrew Knott
Topics: aging, death, friendship, work

BLANK CHECK

Given a blank check by an escaped convict who runs over his bike, young Preston seizes his opportunity to make his wishes come true and fills it out for a million dollars. The resulting orgy of wild, eleven-year-old indulgence delights young viewers, while showing that money can't buy happiness (parents will like this). Throw in some bad guys, a bully, and a beautiful girl and it's a winner.

One in a million!

1994 92m PG B+

Audience: school-age to adults
Content: mild violence, language
Director: Rupert Wainwright
Lead Cast: Brian Bonsall, Karen Duffy, Miguel Ferrer, James Rebhorn, Tone Loc
Topics: ethics, family, friendship, work

BLIND SPOT

When an accident claims the life of her head-of-staff/son-in-law and injures her pregnant daughter, a high-energy congresswoman must face the shock of their drug abuse. Superbly believable story of an overbearing but well-meaning woman who finds she doesn't have the power to fix everything.

See it!

1993 99m PG-13 TVM A+

Audience: adolescents to adults
Content: adult themes, intense dramatic themes
Director: Michael Toshiyuki Uno
Lead Cast: Joanne Woodward, Fritz Weaver, Laura Linney, Reed Diamond
Topics: death, family, parenting

BOPHA!

A black sergeant in the South African police in 1980 finds himself and his worldview at odds with his son, who joins the youth movement against apartheid. Gradually the father comes to see that he can no longer support the status quo. If apartheid had not been abolished, it would be difficult to view this film without despair.

Arresting drama.

1993 114m PG-13 A-

Audience: adults
Content: graphic violence, very rough language, intense dramatic scenes, nudity
Director: Morgan Freeman
Lead Cast: Danny Glover, Maynard Eziashi, Alfre Woodard, Malcolm McDowell, Marius Weyers, Malick Bowens
Topics: children, death, family, friendship, heroism, prejudice, war

BOY WHO COULD FLY, THE

A preteen boy copes with the death of his parents by creating a fantasy world in which he can fly. Soon he is befriended by a family with its own problems. Although this might sound like a depressing story, the movie handles the tale with charm and heart, and the ending is uplifting.

Take off with it.

1986 116m PG A-

Audience: school-age to adults
Content: intense dramatic scenes
Director: Nick Castle
Lead Cast: Jay Underwood, Lucy Deakins, Bonnie Bedelia
Topics: adolescence, death, disability, family, parenting

BREAKING HOME TIES

This superb movie, inspired by Norman Rockwell's paintings, is one of the most sensitively told coming-of-age stories ever on television. Set in rural 1950s Texas, it follows the lives of a dying mother, her tender husband, and their sensitive but naive son, who gets more than a textbook education at college. Also known as *Norman Rockwell's Breaking Home Ties.*

Great cast, wonderful story!

1992 92m NR TVM A

Audience: adolescents to adults
Content: adult themes, language
Director: John Wilder
Lead Cast: Jason Robards, Eva Marie Saint, Doug McKeon, Erin Gray, Claire Trevor
Topics: adolescence, children, death, family, marriage, parenting, romance

BREATHING LESSONS

Ira, a laid-back realist, and Maggie, his meddling, optimistic wife of twenty-nine years, drive to a funeral, visit an estranged ex-daughter-in-law, and return home. *Breathing Lessons* is not action-packed, but it's a full and rewarding, intimate look at mature love and commitment. Presented with warmth and humor by a sterling cast, this film does credit to Ann Tyler's Pulitzer Prize-winning novel.

A breath of fresh air from Hallmark.

1994 98m NR TVM A

Audience: adolescents to adults
Content: nothing objectionable
Director: John Erman
Lead Cast: James Garner, Joanne Woodward, Eileen Heckart, Paul Winfield, Joyce Van Patten
Topics: family, friendship, marriage

BRIEF HISTORY OF TIME, A

Thoughtful movie lovers will treasure this terrific documentary about British physicist Stephen Hawking, who, with the help of computers and personal assistants, overcame the limitations of Lou Gehrig's disease to explore the wonders and perplexities of the universe. Morris's filmic vision marvelously shuttles the audience back and forth between cosmic scope and personal mortality. Based on Hawking's book of the same title.

A filmic journey through space and time.

1992 78m G A American/British

Audience: mature teens and adults
Content: nothing objectionable
Director: Errol Morris
Lead Cast: Stephen Hawking, his colleagues and family
Topics: aging, death, disability, religion, work

CHRISTY

A teenage girl in the early years of the 20th century leaves the safety of her home in Asheville to teach at a mission school in rural Appalachia. This wonderful pilot to the TV series is based on the characters from the popular Catherine Marshall book about her grandmother's real experience in the Smoky Mountains.

Inspiring tale of faith and commitment!

1994 92m NR TVM A-

Audience: school-age to adults
Content: mild violence, intense dramatic scenes
Director: Michael Rhodes
Lead Cast: Kellie Martin, Randall Batinkoff, Tyne Daly, Stewart Finlay-McLennan
Topics: children, heroism, nature, religion, work

CINEMA PARADISO

A fatherless young Sicilian boy is mentored by the projectionist in a town after WW II. He witnesses firsthand the impact of the movies on the village and its various people. Eventually he becomes the projectionist and must decide whether to stay in the village or to leave in order to get an education and to pursue other careers.

Best foreign film Oscar.

1988 123m PG A Italian (subtitled or dubbed)

Audience: teenagers to adults
Content: language, adult situations, nudity
Director: Giuseppe Tornatore
Lead Cast: Phillippe Noiret, Jacques Perrin, Salvatore Cascio
Topics: adolescence, aging, death, religion

CITY OF JOY

A disillusioned young surgeon quits his practice and travels to India in search of life's meaning, finding it in the squalid streets of Calcutta. Though determined to leave medicine behind in America, he's challenged to use his skills where they are desperately needed. A British nurse drafts him to serve in her free clinic, where he learns to give of himself and take risks again.

Swayze at his best.

1992 134m PG-13 A+

Audience: adults
Content: language, violence, adult themes
Director: Roland Joffe
Lead Cast: Patrick Swayze, Pauline Collins, Om Puri
Topics: death, ethics, friendship, heroism

CIVIL WAR, THE

Ken Burns's multitape documentary on the American Civil War, originally broadcast in the U.S. on PBS, is a stirring account of the war that not only ripped apart the nation, but also killed more through sickness, disease, and the weather than through battle. Each episode highlights a period in the war, using photographs, drawings, narration, and music to create a marvelous sense of the battle's inherent drama.

A video triumph.

1989 (9 tapes) appx. 70m ea. NR A+

Audience: adolescents to adults
Content: adult themes
Director: Ken Burns
Lead Cast: (narrator) David McCullough
Topics: heroism, war

CIVIL WAR DIARY

A nine-year-old boy grows into manhood during the Civil War. Too young to fight beside his brothers, he takes their place on the farm with his father until he must take his father's place, too. Meanwhile, he is haunted by the memory of his sister's death at the hands of a masked rider. This film handles the subject of war and hatred sensitively and delivers a message of family love and loyalty. Based on the acclaimed novel *Across Five Aprils*.

Impressive story of courage and commitment.

1991 82m NR B

Audience: adolescents to adults
Content: intense dramatic scenes
Director: Kevin Meyer
Lead Cast: Todd Duffy, Miriam Byrd-Nethery, Hollis McCarthy
Topics: adolescence, death, ethics, family, friendship, war

CLEAR AND PRESENT DANGER

A naive but ethical CIA agent is thrust into the international drug war when he investigates the killing of a friend of the President of the U.S. There is enough action, suspense, and moral nuance in this thriller to entertain most audiences, although the story greatly stretches credulity toward the end. Based on the Tom Clancy novel.

Ford, fear, and fun!

1994 135m PG-13 A-

Audience: teens to adults
Content: graphic violence, language
Director: Phillip Noyce
Lead Cast: Harrison Ford, James Earl Jones, Robert Ritter
Topics: ethics, heroism, war, work

COLD SASSY TREE

This is a television adaptation of Olive Ann Burns's story about an elderly man and a younger woman who marry in the turn-of-the-century South. When suddenly widowed, he quickly announces his intent to wed, for "convenience," the local milliner, who is both surprised and delighted. As the town gossips and condemns, the couple begins falling in love.

Excellent literary adaptation.

1989 100m NR TVM A-

Audience: teens to adults
Content: adult themes and intense dramatic scenes
Director: Joan Tewkesbury
Lead Cast: Faye Dunaway, Richard Widmark, Neil Patrick Harris
Topics: aging, death, marriage, prejudice, romance

COOL RUNNINGS

Four unlikely athletes persuade a disgraced former bobsledder to whip them into shape to compete as Jamaica's first Olympic bobsled team. A hilarious example that truth is stranger than fiction. Based on the real story of the 1988 Jamaican bobsled team.

Warm tears of laughter will run down!

1993 96m PG A+

Audience: school-age to adults
Content: language
Director: Jon Turtletaub
Lead Cast: Leon, Doug E. Doug, Rawle D. Lewis, Malik Yoba, John Candy
Topics: ethics, friendship, sports

CORRINA, CORRINA

A dejected widower and his disturbed young daughter rediscover the joy of life when a sensitive, faithful maid enters their lives. A bit offbeat, this subtle movie will appeal primarily to viewers who like interesting characters, superb sets, and wistful directing.

Whoop it up!

1994 110m PG A-

Audience: teens to adults
Content: adult themes
Director: Jessie Nelson
Lead Cast: Whoopi Goldberg, Ray Liotta, Tina Majorino
Topics: death, family, parenting, religion, romance, work

COURAGE MOUNTAIN

The Heidi story is updated in this tale of the teenager's time at an Italian boarding school during WW I and her subsequent struggle to escape an exploitative orphanage and return to Switzerland over the Alps. A bit overly dramatic at times, but still a fine family film with some superb photography and endearing characters.

Climb aboard.

1989 96m PG A- American/French

Audience: all ages
Content: intense dramatic scenes
Director: Christopher Leitch
Lead Cast: Charlie Sheen, Leslie Caron, Joanna Clark,
    Juliette Caton
Topics: family, heroism, romance, war

CRIMES AND MISDEMEANORS

This is a poignant story of a successful and highly regarded ophthalmologist in New York City who saves his reputation and marriage by hiring a professional hit man to kill his increasingly estranged mistress. The story minimizes sensationalism and focuses on the differences between religious and secular answers to sin and guilt. A troubling but insightful film.

Woody Allen's best.

1989 101m PG-13 A-

Audience: adults
Content: language, adult themes
Director: Woody Allen
Lead Cast: Martin Landau, Anjelica Huston, Alan Alda, Woody
    Allen
Topics: ethics, romance, marriage

CROSSING DELANCEY

A lonely young Jewish woman working at a literary bookshop in New York City is courted by a pickle salesman, but she prefers the "uptown" crowd. This is a marvelous romantic comedy with delightful characters, including a Jewish "bubbe" and her matchmaking friend. Although predictable, the story is still convincing because of a first-rate cast and genuine Jewish humor.

To life!

1988 96m PG A-

Audience: teens to adults
Content: adult situations
Director: Joan Micklin Silver
Lead Cast: Amy Irving, Peter Riegert, Jeroen Krabbe
Topics: aging, family, marriage, religion, romance

CRY FREEDOM

A white South African newspaper editor befriends black activist Steve Biko in the 1970s, increasingly challenging the government's version of political events. This is a moving docudrama about apartheid even though it necessarily simplifies a complex situation. Based on the book by Donald Woods.

An inspiring tearjerker.

1987 153m PG A British

Audience: mature teens to adults
Content: language, adult situations
Director: Richard Attenborough
Lead Cast: Kevin Kline, Penelope Wilton, Denzel Washington
Topics: children, death, ethics, heroism, prejudice, religion, work

CRY IN THE DARK, A

A deeply religious Australian couple endures bigotry and mass hysteria when officials and the public refuse to believe that the couple's infant was killed by a wild dog during a vacation outing. The mother is accused of murder and put through a media-saturated trial. Based on actual events, this gripping film is an incredible story of both personal faith and public persecution.

A gripping story.

1988 116m PG-13 A American/Australian

Audience: mature adolescents to adults
Content: adult situations and themes
Director: Fred Schepisi
Lead Cast: Meryl Streep, Sam Neill
Topics: family, marriage, prejudice, religion

CRY IN THE WILD, A

An adolescent boy deals emotionally with his parents' breakup while trying to survive alone in the Pacific Northwest. As he battles animals and the elements, he also overcomes his own anger and disillusionment. A fine coming-of-age film that won numerous awards, including a gold medal from the International Family Film Society. Based on Gary Paulsen's novel *Hatchet*.

A wild-card film.

1990 82m PG A-

Audience: adolescents to adults
Content: frightening scenes
Director: Mark Griffiths
Lead Cast: Jared Rushton, Ned Beatty, Pamela Sue Martin
Topics: adolescence, family, nature, parenting

DAD

A Wall Street financial executive flies home when his mother has a heart attack, only to discover that his aging father cannot care for himself. Suddenly he has to reconsider his family responsibilities as well as his own relationship with his father and his teenage son. A riveting and realistic story about family commitments, love, and grace.

A celebration of fatherhood.

1989 117m PG A

Audience: adolescents to adults
Content: adult situations and themes
Director: Gary David Goldberg
Lead Cast: Jack Lemmon, Ted Danson, Olympia Dukakis
Topics: adolescence, aging, death, family, parenting

DAKOTA

An eighteen-year-old struggling with a troubled past gets a job on a Texas ranch and learns forgiveness and the joy of giving to others. Although the script is a bit choppy and the outcome predictable, the worthwhile themes and solid performances make this an excellent family film.

Terrific family fare, but not for young children.

1988 93m PG B +

Audience: teens to adults
Content: language
Director: Fred Holmes
Lead Cast: Lou Diamond Phillips, Dee Dee Norton
Topics: death, family, friendship, parenting, work

DARK HORSE

After the death of her mother, a teenage girl and her family move from Los Angeles to the rural West. She gets into trouble and is assigned by a judge to weekend work on a horse farm. There she learns about life while her architect father assesses his own role in his daughter's life. Uplifting themes and excellent horse-riding scenes.

Galloping goodness!

1992 98m PG B+

Audience: school-age to adults
Content: intense dramatic scenes
Director: David Hemmings
Lead Cast: Ed Begley, Jr., Mimi Rogers, Ali Meyers
Topics: adolescence, death, disability, family, friendship, work

DAVE

A presidential look-alike is drawn into a conspiracy to impersonate a U.S. president and takes his job more seriously than the chief of staff would like. Ignorant about politics, Dave begins making decisions that are simply right and just, winning the admiration of the cabinet, the country, and the first lady. An uplifting tale that shows that one person can make a difference if he follows his heart.

Delightful comedy of the average "Dave."

1993 106m PG-13 A

Audience: teens to adults
Content: language, adult situations and themes, nudity
Director: Ivan Reitman
Lead Cast: Kevin Kline, Sigourney Weaver, Frank Langella
Topics: children, death, ethics, friendship, marriage, romance

DAY IN OCTOBER, A

Denmark is no longer a safe haven for Jews or the Danes who resist the German occupation. When an injured resister is hidden by a Jewish girl, she and her parents must take a stand against the evil they have tried to ignore.

Don't resist it.

1990 97m PG-13 A- Danish/American

Audience: teens to adults
Content: graphic violence, intense dramatic scenes
Director: Kenneth Madsen
Lead Cast: D. B. Sweeney, Kelly Wolf, Tovah Feldshuh, Daniel Benzali, Ole Lemmeke
Topics: death, friendship, heroism, prejudice, religion, romance, war

DEAD POETS SOCIETY

An unorthodox and highly charismatic English instructor at a Vermont boys' prep school in the 1950s challenges students to "seize the day." This leads to conflict between the instructor and his more traditional colleagues, as well as to tragedy. Very popular and controversial teen pic.

Nominated for four Oscars.

1989 128m PG A

Audience: teens to adults
Content: language, adult themes
Director: Peter Weir
Lead Cast: Robin Williams, Robert Sean Leonard, Ethan Hawke
Topics: adolescence, death, friendship, parenting

DECORATION DAY

A retired Georgia judge reluctantly renews acquaintance with an equally reluctant old friend in order to persuade him to belatedly accept the Congressional Medal of Honor. In the process, both find new meaning in life and deeper understanding of each other. Both Garner and Cobbs give sensitive, believable performances. A well-done film that shows things are not always what they appear to be.

Deserves a medal!

1990 99m NR TVM A

Audience: teens to adults
Content: violence, language, adult themes
Director: Robert Markowitz
Lead Cast: James Garner, Bill Cobbs, Judith Ivey
Topics: death, ethics, family, friendship, romance, war

DENNIS THE MENACE

Young Dennis once again irritates crotchety neighbor George Wilson as well as neighborhood newcomer "Switchblade Sam." Lots of slapstick violence from innocent Dennis, whose character rivals the kid of *Home Alone*. Sam's character may be too frightening for sensitive kids.

You've gotta love it!

1993 95m PG A-

Audience: all ages
Content: violence
Director: Nick Castle
Lead Cast: Walter Matthau, Mason Gamble, Christopher Lloyd
Topics: children, family, friendship

DESERT BLOOM

A thirteen-year-old girl struggles with growing up in an unpredictable home during the dawn of the atomic age. Her mother sees only what she wants to see, her stepfather is an alcoholic WW II hero, and her beloved aunt who comes to visit lets her down, so she runs away from home. Forgiveness and love see her through.

A poignant coming-of-age story.

1986 106m PG A-

Audience: teens to adults
Content: adult themes, language, mild violence
Director: Eugene Corr
Lead Cast: Jon Voight, Annabeth Gish, JoBeth Williams
Topics: adolescence, family, friendship, parenting, romance, war

DIRTY ROTTEN SCOUNDRELS

When a gauche American trespasses with his scam into a sophisticated British con artist's territory on the French Riviera, they go into high-stakes competition over a sweet young lady. The film is a delightful series of escalating cons, with a dizzying array of visual and verbal humor and wonderful teamwork.

Let yourself be taken in!

1988 110m PG A

Audience: adolescents to adults
Content: language, adult themes
Director: Frank Oz
Lead Cast: Steve Martin, Michael Caine, Glenne Headley
Topics: ethics, romance

DOCTOR, THE

An aloof, highly competent surgeon discovers what it's like to be a patient. The film touchingly portrays the emotional surgery the doctor must perform on his own heart to transform his life and work. It's a celebration of life, love, and empathy. Based on Dr. Ed Rosenbaum's own experiences, the film casts many medical professionals.

The right prescription.

1991 123m PG-13 A +

Audience: teens to adults
Content: language, adult themes, intense dramatic scenes
Director: Randa Haines
Lead Cast: William Hurt, Christine Lahti, Elizabeth Perkins
Topics: death, ethics, family, friendship, marriage, religion, work

DOMINICK AND EUGENE

A medical student and his retarded twin lovingly face the cruel realities of life in working-class Pittsburgh. The "normal" brother's profession and growing love interests, and his twin's bittersweet friendship with a coworker on a garbage truck, complicate their relationship as inseparable siblings. Few films have looked more compassionately at mentally handicapped persons.

Brotherhood!

1988 111m PG-13 A-

Audience: adolescents to adults
Content: language, adult situations
Director: Robert M. Young
Lead Cast: Tom Hulce, Ray Liotta, Jamie Lee Curtis
Topics: disability, family, friendship, romance

DRIVING MISS DAISY

An elderly Jewish lady and her black chauffeur overcome racial and ethnic barriers in the Southern U.S. during the late 1940s. Initially the wealthy Miss Daisy resents her son's insistence that she cannot drive, but the woman and her chauffeur share genuineness, personal integrity, and mutual respect. A subtle but heartwarming film that overcomes prejudice with common humanity. Adapted from the play.

Three Oscars!

1989 99m PG A+

Audience: all ages
Content: language
Director: Bruce Beresford
Lead Cast: Jessica Tandy, Morgan Freeman, Dan Aykroyd
Topics: aging, family, friendship, parenting, prejudice, work

D2: THE MIGHTY DUCKS

This sequel to *The Mighty Ducks* follows the team—with a few ringers—into the junior league world championships. When coach Bombay gives more attention to endorsements and high living than to coaching, the Ducks (now Team USA) are shot down. An enthusiastic film about teamwork and priorities.

As good as it's quacked up to be!

1994 100m PG A-

Audience: adolescents to adults
Content: mild violence, language
Director: Sam Weisman
Lead Cast: Emilio Estevez, Michael Tucker, Jan Rubes, Kathryn Erbe
Topics: friendship, sports

EDWARD SCISSORHANDS

This is a remarkable adult fairy tale about a man-made youth whose creator dies before attaching hands. The youth attempts to live a normal life in suburban America with the aid of a sympathetic family whose daughter falls in love with him. But scissor-like hands and his innocent spirit create unfortunate problems.

A marvelous adult fairy tale.

1990 100m PG-13 A-

Audience: mature teens to adults
Content: language, mild violence
Director: Tim Burton
Lead Cast: Johnny Depp, Winona Ryder, Dianne Wiest
Topics: adolescence, prejudice, romance

EFFICIENCY EXPERT, THE

A middle-aged "efficiency expert" in Australia during the 1960s is hired by a small moccasin manufacturer to save the unprofitable business. He discovers a wildly eccentric group of employees who have no interest in increasing productivity, but who enjoy life, especially slotcar racing. This humorous, whimsical film effectively examines the conflicts between dignity and efficiency in modern life. Superbly made.

A witty tale of dignity.

1992 87m PG A- Australian

Audience: teens to adults
Content: language
Director: Mark Joffe
Lead Cast: Anthony Hopkins, Ben Mendelsohn, Toni Collette
Topics: adolescence, ethics, romance, work

EIGHT MEN OUT

This is a terrific dramatization of the infamous "Black Sox" scandal of 1919, when numerous players on the Chicago White Sox were bribed to throw games in the World Series. Period settings are excellent, performances are outstanding, and the script nicely captures the conflicting personal responses to the temptation to throw the game.

A solid hit.

1988 115m PG A-

Audience: adolescents to adults
Content: language
Director: John Sayles
Lead Cast: John Cusack, Clifton James, Michael Lerner
Topics: ethics, work, sports

84 CHARING CROSS ROAD

An American writer and a British bookseller develop a deep friendship through letters for twenty years. This unusual movie is a study of character and friendship. Based on the autobiographical work of Helen Hanff, it links a stuffy Englishman with an expressive young American—all through the written word. Not for all tastes in film, but a joy for those who like subtle and endearing character studies.

A warmly woven tapestry of mutual affection.

1987 100m PG B

Audience: adults
Content: nothing objectionable
Director: David Jones
Lead Cast: Anne Bancroft, Anthony Hopkins
Topics: aging, friendship, religion

EMMA'S SHADOW

In 1930s Denmark, an unhappy eleven-year-old daughter of wealthy but unloving Russian aristocrats fakes her own kidnapping and takes refuge with a lonely sewer worker. By lying to her host, she is able to stay underground and even to beat the police. The friendship that develops is a stirring statement on the importance of parental love.

Best Danish film of 1988.

1988 97m NR A- Danish (subtitled)

Audience: adults
Content: language
Director: Soren Kragh-Jacobsen
Lead Cast: Line Kruse, Borje Ahstedt
Topics: adolescence, aging, family, friendship, parenting

ENCHANTED APRIL

Two middle-aged, middle-class women from London join a snooty dowager and a wealthy temptress on an April holiday at an Italian villa. Initially the unlikely foursome tangles over personal space and daily schedules, but the springtime setting increasingly enchants their hearts. As guests arrive, spring creates a marvelous mood of utter delight.

Enchanting!

1992 94m PG A

Audience: all ages
Content: mild language
Director: Mike Newell
Lead Cast: Joan Plowright, Miranda Richardson, Polly Walker
Topics: aging, friendship, marriage, romance

ERNEST GREEN STORY, THE

A black teenager leads a small, courageous group to challenge racism in pursuit of their dream of better education in the segregated South in 1954. Green was among the first to take advantage of the Supreme Court desegregation ruling. His story is a testimony to respect, courage, and determination in the face of violent hatred and prejudice.

A historical docudrama.

1993 105m NR A-

Audience: adolescents to adults
Content: violence, intense dramatic scenes
Director: Eric Lanueville
Lead Cast: Morris Chestnut, Ossie Davis
Topics: family, friendship, heroism, prejudice

ETHAN FROME

In turn-of-the-century New England, an emotionally starved husband tries to find happiness in a doomed adulterous relationship with a relative of his hypochondriac wife. A well-crafted, moving story about love and commitment, based on the classic novel by Edith Wharton. Too gloomy for some viewers.

A sobering tragedy.

1993 107m PG A-

Audience: teens to adults
Content: adult situations and themes
Director: John Madden
Lead Cast: Liam Neeson, Joan Allen, Patricia Arquette
Topics: disability, friendship, marriage, religion, romance

FAR AND AWAY

A poor young tenant farmer and his rich landlord's daughter escape Ireland together to find new lives in America. The temporary alliance becomes a necessity for survival in the rough town of Boston. Joseph finds success and a growing bankroll in the boxing ring, while Shannon must swallow her pride and dirty her hands for the first time. Both are driven by the dream of owning their own land in the vast West.

Breathtaking excitement.

1992 140m PG-13 B+

Audience: adults
Content: language, violence, adult situations and themes, intense dramatic scenes, nudity
Director: Ron Howard
Lead Cast: Tom Cruise, Nicole Kidman, Robert Prosky
Topics: family, friendship, romance, work

FAR OFF PLACE, A

When their parents are killed by poachers, two teenagers flee into the Kalahari Desert, guided by a Bushman—their only hope for survival. A good balance of danger and innocent romance, set against the African sky with a Bushman matchmaker, make this a unique coming-of-age film. Fabulous cinematography!

Splendid!

1993 105m PG A-

Audience: teens to adults
Content: violence, intense dramatic scenes
Director: Mikael Salomon
Lead Cast: Reese Witherspoon, Ethan Randall, Maximilian Schell, Jack Thompson, Sarel Bok
Topics: adolescence, death, friendship, nature

FATHER OF THE BRIDE

An upper-middle-class father learns the hard way that daughters' weddings can be costly, elaborate, and highly emotional. Martin delivers the right amount of humor and sensitivity for an enjoyable story. Capture the tension a father feels between his protective instincts and pride over the woman his daughter has become.

Humorous remake of the Spencer Tracy classic.

1991 100m PG B+

Audience: teens to adults
Content: language, adult themes
Director: Charles Shyer
Lead Cast: Steve Martin, Diane Keaton, Kimberly Williams
Topics: family, marriage, parenting, romance

FAT MAN AND LITTLE BOY

An ambitious physicist (Robert Oppenheimer) and an army colonel clash in New Mexico during WW II over the design and production of the first atomic bomb. This is a superb dramatization of actual people and events behind the creation of the most powerful and frightening type of weapon ever made.

An explosive drama.

1989 123m PG-13 A-

Audience: adults
Content: very rough language, adult situations
Director: Roland Joffe
Lead Cast: Paul Newman, Dwight Schultz, Bonnie Bedelia
Topics: ethics, family, war, work

FIELD, THE

Bull McCabe will do almost anything to purchase the land he's worked and nurtured for years as a tenant, and when an "outsider" stands in his way, the land becomes a dark obsession, leading to violence. This tragic drama is full of rich characters, lush scenery, and dark secrets, which surface to destroy a cherished dream. Thought provoking and extremely well done.

Powerful!

1991 113m PG-13 A British

Audience: adults
Content: language, violence, adult themes, intense dramatic scenes
Director: Jim Sheridan
Lead Cast: Richard Harris, Tom Berenger, John Hurt
Topics: death, ethics, family, friendship, religion, work

FIELD OF DREAMS

A modern-day "Noah" ignores the taunts of his neighbors and builds a baseball diamond in the middle of his Iowa cornfield. When he hears a voice saying "If you build it, he will come" he takes a leap of faith that not only brings past baseball greats back to life, but sends him on a journey into his past. Along the way he finds understanding, reconciliation, and redemption.

A magical adult fantasy!

1989 106m PG A-

Audience: adolescents to adults
Content: language
Director: Phil Alden Robinson
Lead Cast: Kevin Costner, Amy Madigan, James Earl Jones, Burt Lancaster, Ray Liotta, Timothy Busfield
Topics: family, friendship, sports

FLINTSTONES, THE

When he's promoted at the quarry, Fred is duped into embezzling and loses his best friend. This reversal into live action is even more clever than the popular cartoon series. It works for all age levels and nostalgically re-creates the cartoon's opening and closing sequences.

Yabba dabba do it!

1994 92m PG B+

Audience: all ages
Content: nothing objectionable
Director: Brian Levant
Lead Cast: John Goodman, Elizabeth Perkins, Rick Moranis, Rosie O'Donnell, Elizabeth Taylor, Kyle MacLachlan
Topics: ethics, family, friendship, work

FOREVER YOUNG

An Air Force test pilot in the 1930s is secretly "frozen" after his near fiancée becomes comatose following a vehicle accident. Fifty years later, he is accidentally "thawed" and finds out that his former love is still alive. As he searches for her, he is also sought by the military and plagued by health problems. A young boy and his mother help him to avoid the authorities and to find his love.

Old-style romance.

1992 114m PG A-

Audience: adolescents to adults
Content: mild violence, nudity
Director: Steve Miner
Lead Cast: Mel Gibson, Isabel Glasser, Elijah Wood, Jamie Lee Curtis
Topics: aging, death, friendship, romance

FORTUNES OF WAR

This superb British TV miniseries follows a young couple trying to live normally in Europe and northern Africa during WW II. As their marriage and careers are battered by the war, they still find love and forgiveness amidst hardship and even death. Terrific performances and photography—a splendid adaptation of the novels by Olivia Manning.

A BBC masterpiece.

1987 330m NR TVM A British/American

Audience: teens to adults
Content: language, violence, adult situations and themes
Director: James Cellan Jones
Lead Cast: Kenneth Branagh, Emma Thompson, Ronald Pickup
Topics: death, ethics, marriage, religion, war

FOXFIRE

An elderly widow in the Blue Ridge Mountains talks to the spirit of her husband as she contemplates the future of the family land sought by a developer. Her son, a successful country singer, comes home to perform and to talk his mother into selling the land and moving near him. Hallmark version of the Broadway production.

Emmy Award to Tandy.

1987 100m PG TVM B+

Audience: school-age to adults
Content: language
Director: Jud Taylor
Lead Cast: Jessica Tandy, Hume Cronyn, John Denver
Topics: aging, family, parenting

FREE WILLY

A homeless twelve-year-old boy finds new meaning in life when he develops a special relationship with a 7,000-pound whale at a sea park. Some terrific cinematography and careful directing make this a believable and inspiring story for the whole family.

A boy and his whale.

1993 105m PG A-

Audience: school-age to adults
Content: potentially frightening to preschoolers
Director: Simon Wincer
Lead Cast: Jason James Richter, Lori Petty, Michael Madsen
Topics: adolescence, ethics, family, friendship, heroism, nature, parenting

FRIED GREEN TOMATOES

A repressed, middle-aged Southern woman meets an elderly, free-spirited spinster in a nursing home and listens to her tales of youth. Wacky and offbeat, sometimes shocking and troubling, but also charming and hopeful about life. Based on Fanny Flagg's novel (Flagg also has a cameo).

Warm and spicy!

1991 128m PG-13 A-

Audience: adults
Content: violence, adult situations and themes, language, intense dramatic scenes
Director: Jon Avnet
Lead Cast: Mary Stuart Masterson, Jessica Tandy, Kathy Bates
Topics: aging, death, ethics, family, friendship, prejudice

FRIENDSHIP IN VIENNA, A

As Hitler extends his control to Austria, two teenage girls, one Jewish and one Catholic, are torn apart. Their deep friendship enables them to risk their lives for each other in defiance of their families. A mature, moving portrait based on the book *Devil in Vienna* by Doris Orgel. Ed Asner at his richest.

A finely orchestrated piece.

1988 100m NR TVM A

Audience: adolescents to adults
Content: violence, intense dramatic scenes
Director: Arthur Allan Seidelman
Lead Cast: Edward Asner, Jane Alexander, Stephen Macht, Jenny Lewis, Kamie Harper, Rosemary Forsyth
Topics: death, ethics, family, friendship, prejudice, religion

FUGITIVE, THE

A shrewd doctor, wrongfully convicted of killing his wife, escapes federal custody and searches in Chicago for the real murderer while agents close in on him. A real thriller with excellent special effects, a haunting sound track, and uncanny performances by Ford and Jones. Based on the TV series.

Track it down!

1993 124m PG-13 A

Audience: teens to adults
Content: violence, language, intense dramatic scenes
Director: Andrew Davis
Lead Cast: Harrison Ford, Tommy Lee Jones, Sela Ward
Topics: ethics, friendship

GETTYSBURG

The convictions of noble men on both sides of the Civil War lead them into the costliest battle in American history. Well-documented and authentic epic of this tragic battle, stunningly filmed. Shows unusual insight into the minds and motives of these men. Especially touching is the portrayal of the teacher, Chamberlain, who showed compassion and courage in the face of overwhelming odds.

An absorbing, moving tribute.

1993 254m PG A

Audience: teens to adults
Content: graphic violence, language
Director: Ronald Maxwell
Lead Cast: Tom Berenger, Martin Sheen, C. Thomas Howell, Richard Jordan, Jeff Daniels, Sam Elliott, Maxwell Caulfield
Topics: death, heroism, war

GIRL OF THE LIMBERLOST, A

In 1908 in rural Indiana, a teenage girl struggles between attending the city high school and helping her widowed mother on the farm. Based on the book by Gene Stratton Porter, the movie sensitively captures the tension between human hopes and the reality of work and pain. WonderWorks presentation.

A great find.

1990 104m NR TVM A-

Audience: adolescents to adults
Content: adult themes
Director: Burt Brinckerhoff
Lead Cast: Annette O'Toole, Joanna Cassidy, Heather Fairfield
Topics: adolescence, family, friendship, nature

GLASS MENAGERIE, THE

An aging Southern belle teeters between memories of her glamorous past and manipulation of her children's future. The film is a haunting treatment of Tennessee Williams's classic play, with fine characterizations, especially by Malkovich as the troubled son, Tom. A fine example of film adaptation from the stage.

Sensitive and sad classic.

1987 134m PG A

Audience: teens to adults
Content: language, adult themes
Director: Paul Newman
Lead Cast: Joanne Woodward, John Malkovich, Karen Allen
Topics: family, parenting, romance

GODS MUST BE CRAZY II, THE

In this delightfully offbeat comedy, a bushman, his children, animal poachers, warring factions, a successful businesswoman and others converge in a crazy story that takes place in the African outback. It's hard not to like such a whimsical tale, especially when it's told with compassion for mankind. Sequel to *The Gods Must Be Crazy*.

Human beings are nutty!

1989 96m PG A- American/Botswanian

Audience: all ages
Content: language
Director: Jamie Uys
Lead Cast: N!xau, Lena Farugia, Hans Strydom
Topics: children, family, parenting, war

GOODBYE, MISS 4TH OF JULY

The selfless daughter of hardworking Greek immigrants experiences romance, disease, and especially prejudice in West Virginia before WW I. This true-life story wonderfully captures the commitment and generous spirit of so many American immigrants, with ample doses of Disney's inspirational movie magic.

Hello, sweet movie!

1988 87m NR TVM B +

Audience: adolescents to adults
Content: adult themes
Director: George Miller
Lead Cast: Louis Gossett, Jr., Chris Sarandon, Roxana Zal
Topics: death, ethics, family, friendship, prejudice, romance, work

GORILLAS IN THE MIST

A woman's dedication to researching the mountain gorilla leads to an obsession with protecting them from extinction at any cost. Based on the true story of Dian Fossey's twenty years in Rwanda's remote jungle, it is a beautifully photographed film. Many stirring scenes of authentic interaction between the gorillas and their researcher/protector.

A courageous film.

1988 129m PG-13 B +

Audience: adults
Content: very rough language, adult situations and themes, intense dramatic scenes
Director: Michael Apted
Lead Cast: Sigourney Weaver, Bryan Brown, Julie Harris
Topics: death, ethics, friendship, nature, romance, war, work

GREEN CARD

To remain in the U.S., a French tourist enters into a "paper" marriage with a horticulturalist who has her own reason to accept the arrangement. Both get more than they bargained for when immigration officials become suspicious. In order to convince authorities that their marriage is valid, they must learn everything they can about each other in two days. Totally contrived, but marvelously told.

A delightful romantic comedy.

1990 106m PG-13 A- Australian/French

Audience: adolescents to adults
Content: language, adult themes
Director: Peter Weir
Lead Cast: Gérard Depardieu, Andie MacDowell
Topics: ethics, marriage, romance

GROUNDHOG DAY

A cynical, sarcastic TV weatherman in Pittsburgh travels to Punxatawney to cover the annual Groundhog Day ceremonies. He awakes in a local bed-and-breakfast hotel the next day only to discover that he is reliving the previous day. As the months go by, with him reliving a new Groundhog Day over and over again, he worries that he might never see "tomorrow" again.

Scrooge arrives in Punxatawney!

1993 108m PG B+

Audience: adolescents to adults
Content: language, violence
Director: Harold Ramis
Lead Cast: Bill Murray, Andie MacDowell
Topics: death, romance

GUILTY BY SUSPICION

A successful Hollywood movie director in 1951 faces blacklisting if he doesn't cooperate with the public investigation of Communists led by a congressional committee. Faced with an end to his career, he reexamines his life, including his relationships with a young son and an estranged wife. Oversimplification of the McCarthy era in America, but a sensitive look at personal ethics and family life.

A moving tale of integrity.

1991 103m PG-13 A-

Audience: mature teens to adults
Content: language, adult situations and themes
Director: Irwin Winkler
Lead Cast: Robert De Niro, Annette Bening, George Wendt
Topics: ethics, family, friendship, marriage, parenting, work

HAMLET

Shakespeare's Hamlet seeks revenge for the murder of his father in this compelling adaptation by gifted director Franco Zeffirelli. Gibson's performance is excellent, the setting and cinematography are superb, and the story moves energetically toward its tragic conclusion. This is the most accessible version of *Hamlet* on tape—an outstanding introduction for those unfamiliar with the play.

Give it welcome, Horatio!

1990 135m PG A-

Audience: adolescents to adults
Content: violence
Director: Franco Zeffirelli
Lead Cast: Mel Gibson, Glenn Close, Alan Bates
Topics: death, ethics, family, friendship

HEAVEN AND EARTH

In 16th-century Japan, two warlords fight proudly after the emperor loses control of the land. One is driven to battle by a sense of loyalty and divine destiny, the other by ambition and the desire for power. A remarkable movie that captures the "beautiful" images of carefully orchestrated battles as well as the glory and tragedy of mankind.

Japanese epic.

1990 102m PG-13 A Japanese (subtitled)

Audience: adults
Content: graphic violence, adult themes
Director: Haruki Kadokawa
Lead Cast: Takaai Enoki, Masahiko Tsugawa
Topics: death, heroism, war

HENRY V

This is a stirring cinematic adaptation of Shakespeare's play. King Henry inspires his troops at Agincourt to overcome seemingly insurmountable odds by defeating the French to reclaim his rightful place on the throne. Emphasizes the young king's faith in God and the development of his leadership abilities in the face of self-doubt.

Superb adaptation.

1989 137m PG A British

Audience: adolescents to adults
Content: violence
Director: Kenneth Branagh
Lead Cast: Kenneth Branagh, Paul Scofield, Emma Thompson
Topics: family, heroism, war

HOME ALONE

A precocious eight-year-old defends his home against a pair of bungling burglars when he is inadvertently left behind while his family vacations in Paris. Hilarious, suspenseful, and even touching movie as Kevin takes seriously his responsibility as "man of the house." Though initially Kevin is glad to be rid of his family, in the end he's grateful at their return, and they see him in a new light as well. Lots of slapstick. Better than the sequel.

Don't leave the video store without it.

1990 102m PG A-

Audience: school-age to adults
Content: violence, language
Director: Chris Columbus
Lead Cast: Macaulay Culkin, Joe Pesci, Daniel Stern
Topics: ethics, family, friendship, heroism, religion

HOME OF OUR OWN, A

The "Lacey tribe," a single mom and her six kids, leaves their dead-end life in the city with all their possessions in a rattletrap car and head for a new life in Idaho's wide-open spaces. Together they build and barter their shell of a house into a home, with the help of the church bargain basement, the local salvage yard, and their neighbor, "Mr. Moon." The working-class language may be too offensive for some viewers.

A home with heart.

1993 104m PG A-

Audience: adolescents to adults
Content: mild violence, adult themes, very rough language, intense dramatic scenes
Director: Tony Bill
Lead Cast: Kathy Bates, Edward Furlong, Soon-Teck Oh
Topics: children, family, parenting, prejudice, work

HOMEWARD BOUND:
THE INCREDIBLE JOURNEY

Three beloved pets fear they've been abandoned while being cared for by a friend, and cross the Pacific Northwest wilderness to return home. This fine Disney film is above the usual "pet-lost-in-the-wilderness" film due to the fine animal characterizations, the contemporary dialogue, and the strong message of love and commitment.

An incredible family film.

1993 89m G A

Audience: all ages
Content: intense dramatic scenes
Director: Duwayne Dunham
Lead Cast: (voices) Michael J. Fox, Sally Field, Don Ameche
Topics: family, friendship, heroism, nature

HONEY, I BLEW UP THE KID

In this hilarious sequel to *Honey, I Shrunk the Kids*, Wayne zaps his two-year-old into a giant toddler. Baby Adam wreaks havoc on the house and the neighborhood before heading for the big time in Las Vegas. While the Szalinskis try to shrink Adam, Wayne's superior calls in the military. Meanwhile, Adam's "big" brother is trapped with the baby-sitter in Adam's pocket in this delightful comedy.

Hugely entertaining.

1992 89m PG A

Audience: school-age to adults
Content: intense dramatic scenes
Director: Randall Kleiser
Lead Cast: Rick Moranis, Marcia Strassman, Daniel/Joshua Shalikar
Topics: adolescence, children, family, friendship, parenting

HONEY, I SHRUNK THE KIDS

Four kids are shrunk to the size of a pinhead when they cross the path of an experimental ray gun invented by their eccentric father whose experiments usually backfire. When this one finally works it lands the four squabbling kids in a fight for their lives to cross the backyard to safety, as they battle giant bees, the lawnmower, and the family dog. Great special effects! Sequel—*Honey, I Blew Up the Kid.*

A honey of a family film.

1989 93m PG A

Audience: school-age to adults
Content: intense dramatic scenes
Director: Joe Johnston
Lead Cast: Rick Moranis, Amy O'Neill, Robert Oliveri
Topics: adolescence, family, friendship, heroism, nature, romance

HOOK

Captain Hook returns to the Peter Pan story to get back at a grown-up Peter, who has become a successful businessman in America. Hook takes Peter's children hostage, and Peter can save them only by returning to Never-Never Land and battling the evil Hook. The problem is, Peter has forgotten his former life and must regain his belief and his childlike sense of imagination and innocence to succeed.

Believe it!

1991 135m PG B+

Audience: all ages
Content: mild violence and intense dramatic scenes
Director: Steven Spielberg
Lead Cast: Dustin Hoffman, Robin Williams, Maggie Smith
Topics: family, heroism, parenting, work

HOOSIERS

A tiny Indiana high school has barely enough players for a basketball team, but its mysterious new coach turns this motley group into a championship team. This heartwarming story combines the thrill of high school basketball with rich characterizations. Not only is a team reborn, but so are hope and love in many of the townspeople, from the town drunk to the skeptical assistant principal and the new coach.

Go, team!

1987 114m PG A

Audience: adolescents to adults
Content: language
Director: David Anspaugh
Lead Cast: Gene Hackman, Barbara Hershey, Dennis Hopper
Topics: friendship, romance, sports

HOWARD'S END

Two British families in turn-of-the-century England struggle to make their dreams real. An upper-class family seeks wealth and status, while a middle-class family seeks happiness. When the two families are joined through marriage, members clash over honesty and integrity. The result is a tapestry of broken hearts and ill-fated dreams. A moving portrait of human nature.

Nominated for 8 Academy Awards.

1992 137m PG A- British

Audience: adults
Content: adult situations and themes
Director: James Ivory
Lead Cast: Anthony Hopkins, Vanessa Redgrave, Helena Bonham
Topics: family, marriage, prejudice, romance

HUCK AND THE KING OF HEARTS

A contemporary "Huck" flees his abusive stepfather and joins up
with "Jim," a Native American ex-con. Pursued by Huck's loving
mom, an offbeat aunt, and a murderous drug dealer, they head for
Huck's legendary grandfather in Las Vegas. A funny, touching movie
about self-discovery and friendship.

Heartwarming adventure!

1993 103m PG B +

Audience: adolescents to adults
Content: mild violence
Director: Michael Keusch
Lead Cast: Chauncey Leopardi, Graham Greene, Dee Wallace
Stone, Joe Piscopo, Gretchen Hecker, John Astin
Topics: ethics, family, friendship, heroism, prejudice

HUNT FOR RED OCTOBER, THE

An American intelligence pro tries to aid the captain of a secret
new Soviet nuclear sub who apparently wants to defect to the West
during the craft's maiden voyage. The captain has to outfox other
Soviet ships and watch for mutinous opposition on the sub. Meanwhile, the American has to predict what the Soviet captain will do.
Based on Tom Clancy's novel.

Riveting thriller.

1990 135m PG B +

Audience: adolescents to adults
Content: language, violence
Director: John McTiernan
Lead Cast: Sean Connery, Alec Baldwin, Scott Glenn
Topics: heroism, war

I'LL FLY AWAY: THEN AND NOW

The civil rights era is revisited through sixty-three-year-old Lilly, who passes on her memories and insights to her twelve-year-old grandson. Her fictional story poignantly incorporates real events and reminds viewers of injustice, courage, and forgiveness. Starts off slowly, but worth the wait.

Soaring drama!

1993 90m NR TVM A-

Audience: adolescents to adults
Content: mild violence, adult themes, language, intense dramatic scenes
Director: Jan Sander
Lead Cast: Sam Waterston, Regina Taylor, Bill Cobbs, Rae'ven Kelly, Jason London, Ashlee Levitch, John Aaron Bennett, Peter Simmons
Topics: family, heroism, prejudice

INCIDENT, THE

During WW II, a small-town attorney in Colorado is forced by a federal judge to defend a German soldier from a nearby POW camp accused of killing an American doctor. A superb script and Matthau's excellent performance transform this story into a shining testimony to justice and truth. A good antidote to political correctness of all kinds.

Matthau's TV-movie debut.

1989 98m NR TVM A-

Audience: teens to adults
Content: language
Director: Joseph Sargent
Lead Cast: Walter Matthau, Harry Morgan, Robert Carradine
Topics: death, ethics, family, heroism, prejudice, war, work

INTO THE WEST

Two young boys escape the tenements of Belfast on a beautiful white horse, planning to live as cowboys in "the West" they've seen on TV. The fantastic horse, a gift from their Gypsy grandfather, protects them from danger while leading them and their father, who searches for them, back to their roots. Based on Michael Pearce's story rich with myth and fantasy.

Take a fantastic journey.

1993 97m PG A- Ireland

Audience: adolescents to adults
Content: intense dramatic scenes
Director: Mike Newell
Lead Cast: Gabriel Byrne, Ellen Barkin, Ruaidhri Conroy, Ciaran Fitzgerald, David Kelly
Topics: death, ethics, family, friendship, parenting, prejudice

IRON WILL

After losing his father in a freak dogsled accident, a seventeen-year-old boy enters the team in a grueling race for a $10,000 prize. All odds are against him, but Will needs to win or his mother will lose the farm. For all the right reasons, as well as the self-serving attentions of a newsman, he becomes America's hero.

Inspiring tale of indomitable courage.

1994 110m PG A+

Audience: adolescents to adults
Content: mild violence, intense dramatic scenes
Director: Charles Haid
Lead Cast: Mackenzie Astin, Kevin Spacey, David Ogden Stiers, George Gerdes
Topics: heroism, nature

JEAN DE FLORETTE

A proud, aging French farmer conspires with a dim-witted nephew to drive a neighboring farmer out of business by plugging the spring that delivers water to the area. Driven by selfish ambition and the nephew's dream of growing carnations, they succeed. Story continues in *Manon of the Spring*. Based on Marcel Pagnol's novel.

Superb tale of greed.

1986 122m PG A French (subtitled)

Audience: mature teens to adults
Content: mild language
Director: Claude Berri
Lead Cast: Yves Montand, Gérard Depardieu
Topics: ethics, religion, work

JOURNEY OF HOPE

A poor Kurdish couple leaves six of their seven children behind in Turkey to emigrate illegally to Switzerland in the hope of a better life. Though arrangements have been made in advance, once on their way they are at the mercy of "contacts" who eventually strip them of all their possessions. When there is nothing left, they are abandoned with fellow émigrés to make their own way across the mountains.

Fact-based, emotionally gripping journey.

1991 111m PG B Swiss (subtitled)

Audience: adults
Content: language, violence, intense dramatic scenes
Director: Xavier Koller
Lead Cast: Necmettin Cobanoglu, Nur Surer, Emin Sivas
Topics: death, ethics, family, work

JURASSIC PARK

An eccentric elderly man creates a dinosaur "park" on an island off the coast of Costa Rica by re-creating prehistoric DNA from the blood of fossilized mosquitoes. When a small group of people, including several children, is invited to visit the park prior to its public opening, they are plunged into a frightening battle between man and beast. Based on Michael Crichton's novel.

Spielbergian magic.

1993 140m PG-13 B+

Audience: adolescents to adults
Content: language, violence, intense dramatic scenes
Director: Steven Spielberg
Lead Cast: Sam Neill, Laura Dern, Jeff Goldblum
Topics: children, ethics, nature

KING OF THE HILL

An adolescent boy becomes a man in Depression-era St. Louis when he is left to manage on his own. Living in a run-down hotel, he dodges the cruel manager and forms a network of odd, similarly bereft friends. He develops courage and generosity as he struggles to reunite his scattered family.

A rich character drama.

1993 103m PG-13 A-

Audience: teens to adults
Content: mild violence, adult situations, language, intense dramatic scenes
Director: Steven Soderbergh
Lead Cast: Jesse Bradford, Jeroen Krabbé, Adrien Brody, Lisa Eichhorn, Spalding Gray, Karen Allen, Elizabeth McGovern
Topics: adolescence, family, prejudice, work

LAND BEFORE TIME, THE

A group of five orphaned baby dinosaurs of different species help each other through a perilous journey from their now barren homeland to a fabled green valley. Bluth's animation rivals Disney, and characters are developed sensitively. The beginning may be too sad for small viewers, but all ends well.

You've gotta love these babies!

1988 69m G B+ Animated

Audience: all ages
Content: intense dramatic scenes
Director: Don Bluth
Lead Cast: (voices) Pat Hingle, Gabriel Damon, Helen Shaver
Topics: children, death, family, friendship, heroism, nature

LANTERN HILL

A twelve-year-old Canadian girl in the Depression tries to bring together her separated parents after years of family problems and misunderstandings. Magnificent scenery and endearing characters create a sensitive story of grace overcoming fear and guilt.

Green Gables revisited.

1990 108m NR TVM A- Canadian

Audience: adolescents to adults
Content: nothing objectionable
Director: Kevin Sullivan
Lead Cast: Sam Waterston, Marion Bennett, Sarah Polley
Topics: adolescence, family, parenting

LASSIE

A contemporary family leaves Baltimore to return to the bucolic family farm in Virginia. Along the way they pick up Lassie, who joins the troubled adolescent son in a series of humorous and mildly frightening adventures on the farm. Lassie fans will cheer this contemporary movie "starring" the great-great-great-great-great-grandson of the collie who played the part in the wonderful *Lassie Come Home* (1943).

Bring *Lassie* home!

1994 91m PG A-

Audience: school-age to adults
Content: mild violence
Director: Dan Petrie
Lead Cast: Thomas Guiry, Helen Slater, Jon Tenney, Richard Farnsworth
Topics: children, death, family, friendship, parenting, work

LEAGUE OF THEIR OWN, A

While the men are at war, a remarkable group of young women keep baseball alive in 1943 by joining the All-American Girls Professional Baseball League. Their coach is an obnoxious drunk, the pay is lousy, fans are rude, and travel prevents a decent family life. Nevertheless, these women play their hearts out. An endearing film about an overlooked chapter of American history.

Based on a true story.

1992 100m PG B +

Audience: adolescents to adults
Content: language, adult themes
Director: Penny Marshall
Lead Cast: Geena Davis, Tom Hanks, Madonna
Topics: friendship, marriage, sports, war

LEAN ON ME

Freeman excels as "crazy" Joe Clark, the authoritarian principal of a New Jersey high school who carries a bullhorn and a baseball bat and chains the doors to keep out "losers." Based on real events, the story is an inspiring look at the importance of discipline in the lives of troubled youth.

Tough love.

1989 105m PG-13 A

Audience: teens to adults
Content: language, mild violence
Director: John G. Avildsen
Lead Cast: Morgan Freeman, Beverly Todd, Robert Guillaume
Topics: adolescence, family, parenting, prejudice

LEAP OF FAITH

Con artist Jonas Nightengale pitches his tent and phony salvation in an impoverished Kansas town. With the help of his flirtatious manager, he outmaneuvers the sheriff and outsmarts the "suckers" until a genuine miracle occurs. The energy and foot-stomping music of an old-time tent revival, and an intriguing (if not entirely accurate) peek behind the scenes.

A good show with a lot of hope!

1992 110m PG-13 A-

Audience: teens to adults
Content: adult themes, language
Director: Richard Pearce
Lead Cast: Steve Martin, Debra Winger, Liam Neeson, Lolita Davidovich, Lucas Haas
Topics: ethics, religion, romance

LIFE WITH MIKEY

"Mikey," a has-been child actor-turned-agent, coasts through his shallow life on his reputation until a young pickpocket steals his wallet, his heart, and the show. Angie is a street smart ten-year-old con artist who just needs a little love and understanding—not to mention a few hundred thousand!

Get a life—*Life with Mikey*!

1993 91m PG A-

Audience: school-age to adults
Content: adult themes, language
Director: James Lapine
Lead Cast: Michael J. Fox, Christina Vidal, Nathan Lane, Cyndi Lauper, David Krumholtz
Topics: children, ethics, friendship, parenting, work

LIGHT IN THE JUNGLE, THE

This dramatization of the faithful work of Dr. Albert Schweitzer in his jungle hospital in Africa looks at his struggles with native religions, imperialist Europeans, and bureaucratic medical experts. McDowell's convincing performance and some excellent settings make this a compelling account of Schweitzer's altruistic efforts on behalf of African people. A moving tribute to a great humanitarian.

A tropical treasure.

1990 86m PG A-

Audience: adolescents to adults
Content: frightening scenes
Director: Gray Hofmeyr
Lead Cast: Malcolm McDowell, Susan Strasberg, Andrew Davis
Topics: heroism, nature, prejudice, religion

LION, THE WITCH, AND THE WARDROBE, THE (THE CHRONICLES OF NARNIA)

When four children walk through the door of a strange wardrobe in England, they find themselves in the world of Narnia, where they must aid Aslan the lion to defeat the evil White Witch. True to C. S. Lewis's work, this British film is a delightful telling of the children's adventures as kings and queens in Narnia, where animals speak, mythical creatures roam, and danger lurks. WonderWorks.

Enter a magical land.

1988 165m NR TVM B +

Audience: school-age to adults
Content: mild violence
Director: Alex Kirby
Lead Cast: Richard Dempsey, Sophie Cook, Jonathan Scott, Sophie Wilcox
Topics: death, ethics, friendship, heroism, religion, war

LION KING, THE

When the lion prince's father is killed, the cub takes the blame and runs away—until he is summoned back to fulfill his responsibility as king of the pride. Disney blends drama and comedy masterfully in this first animated feature not based on a children's story. Preschoolers may be alternately frightened or bored at times.

A roaring success!

1994 85m G A- Animated

Audience: all ages
Content: mild violence, intense dramatic scenes
Director: Roger Allers, Rob Minkoff
Lead Cast: (voices) Matthew Broderick, James Earl Jones, Jeremy Irons, Robert Guillaume, Whoopi Goldberg, Cheech Marin, Moira Kelly, Jonathan Taylor Thomas
Topics: adolescence, death, friendship

LITTLE BIG LEAGUE

A precocious, fatherless, eleven-year-old boy inherits the Minnesota Twins, takes over as team manager, and leads the major-league prima donnas to the playoffs. Along the way he learns valuable lessons about sport and life. A bit slow-paced and predictable, not to mention totally implausible, but a sure-fire hit with baseball fans young and old. Based on a story by Gregory Pincus.

Every Little Leaguer's dream.

1994 118m PG A-

Audience: all ages
Content: nothing objectionable
Director: Andrew Scheinman
Lead Cast: Luke Edwards, Timothy Busfield, Ashley Crow
Topics: adolescence, children, family, friendship, parenting, sports, work

LITTLE MAN TATE

A seven-year-old child prodigy becomes a student at a special institute for gifted children, while his cocktail waitress mother questions what's right for him. Caught between the cold stimulation of the institute and the warm love of his poorly educated mother, he seems unable to live a normal life. A touching portrait of the joys and perils of giftedness.

A big film.

1991 94m PG A-

Audience: teens to adults
Content: language
Director: Jodie Foster
Lead Cast: Jodie Foster, Harry Connick, Jr., Dianne Wiest
Topics: children, friendship, parenting

LITTLE MERMAID, THE

A stubborn teenage mermaid, longing for a prince, defies her father by trading her beautiful voice for human legs. Unable to speak to the prince she loves, she almost loses him. Fortunately she has friends under the sea. The music won Oscars, and the animation is exceptional. Children love this movie version of the tale by Hans Christian Anderson, though it's very intense at times.

Be a part of this world!

1989 80m G A+ Animated

Audience: all ages
Content: intense dramatic scenes
Director: John Musker, Ron Clemente
Lead Cast: (voices) Jodi Benson, Pat Carroll, Samuel E. Wright
Topics: adolescence, heroism, parenting, romance

LITTLE PRINCESS, A

Wealthy Sara Crewe elicits jealousy but also wins friends at an exclusive boarding school in Victorian England. Her father's death leaves her penniless and changes the course of her life. Based on the classic by Frances Hodgson Burnett, *A Little Princess* is destined to become a film classic as well.

1990 Parents' Choice Award winner!

1986 176m NR TVM A

Audience: school-age to adults
Content: intense dramatic scenes
Director: Carol Wiseman
Lead Cast: Amelia Shankley, Nigel Havers, Maureen Lipman
Topics: children, death, family, friendship, prejudice

LONESOME DOVE

A pair of aging Texas Rangers embark on the final journey of their lives—a grueling cattle drive across the Northwest. This moving drama is generally considered one of the best TV miniseries of all time, appealing to far more than western buffs. Based on Larry McMurty's novel.

Save it for a long, lonely weekend!

1989 380m NR TVM A

Audience: teens to adults
Content: violence, language, intense dramatic scenes
Director: Simon Wincer
Lead Cast: Robert Duvall, Tommy Lee Jones, Danny Glover, Diane Lane, Robert Ulrich
Topics: aging, death, friendship, nature, work

LONG DAY CLOSES, THE

An adolescent boy in working-class England during the 1950s watches and listens to everyday life. This offbeat, masterfully directed movie without a plot, subtly captures through image and music the curiosity, innocence, and fears of early adolescents, as well as the ambiance of urban Catholic life.

What a day!

1993 82m PG A- British

Audience: teens to adults
Content: adult themes, language
Director: Terence Davies
Lead Cast: Leigh McCormack, Marjorie Yates, Anthony Watson, Aysee Owens
Topics: adolescence, family, parenting, religion

LONG WALK HOME, THE

A dignified black maid and her kindhearted female employer are caught personally in the public conflict over the bus boycott by blacks in Alabama in 1955. This moving portrait of Southern segregation uses some actual film and audio recordings from the period to enhance its historical realism. Terrific performances by Spacek and Goldberg.

Inspiring and moving.

1990 94m PG A

Audience: adolescents to adults
Content: language
Director: Richard Pearce
Lead Cast: Sissy Spacek, Whoopi Goldberg, Dwight Schultz
Topics: family, friendship, marriage, parenting, prejudice

LOOKING FOR MIRACLES

A teenage camp counselor in Canada is forced to bring his younger brother along for the summer. As the summer progresses, the two learn new love and respect for each other amid the crazy shenanigans of a typical camp. Heartwarming vignettes set against a comedic backdrop in the north woods.

Fine family fare.

1991 102m NR A-

Audience: all ages
Content: adult themes
Director: Kevin Sullivan
Lead Cast: Greg Spottiswood, Zachary Bennett
Topics: adolescence, family, friendship

LORENZO'S OIL

Determined parents fight the medical establishment as they seek a cure for their formerly vivacious nine-year-old son, who is struck with a rare, incurable disease. The heartbreaking ravages of adrenoleukodystrophy are graphically portrayed in this emotionally intense film based on a true story.

Inspiring!

1992 110m PG-13 A

Audience: teens to adults
Content: intense dramatic scenes
Director: George Miller
Lead Cast: Susan Sarandon, Nick Nolte, Zach Greenburg
Topics: death, disability, ethics, family, parenting, religion

LOST IN YONKERS

Neil Simon's bittersweet tale follows a year in the life of a teenage boy and his younger brother who stay with their crusty grandmother and whimsical aunt in Yonkers during WW II. Marvelously acted and directed, the movie delicately addresses the hardships of family relations, especially the inability to deal with a harsh past.

A terrific find.

1993 99m PG B+

Audience: teens to adults
Content: language, adult situations and themes
Director: Martha Coolidge
Lead Cast: Richard Dreyfuss, Mercedes Ruehl
Topics: adolescence, aging, family, romance

LUCAS

An exceptional sixteen-year-old boy tries to overcome his unpopularity by winning a girlfriend. Miles above the typical teen flick, this film looks sensitively at the joys and pain of adolescence, including romance. Terrific performances and outstanding direction.

Look at this one.

1986 96m PG-13 A +

Audience: adolescents to adults
Content: language
Director: David Seltzer
Lead Cast: Corey Haim, Charlie Sheen, Kerri Green
Topics: adolescence, family, friendship, romance

MADAME SOUSATZKA

An eccentric piano teacher instructs her promising fifteen-year-old pupil in the piano and in life, while trying to repress her own failure. When his teacher's and mother's goals don't mesh, he learns that he has to make some of his own decisions and risk failure. A warm, rich story with well-developed characters.

See it! Feel it!

1989 117m PG-13 A-

Audience: mature teens to adults
Content: adult themes, language
Director: John Schlesinger
Lead Cast: Shirley MacLaine, Navin Chowdhry, Shabana Azmi, Peggy Ashcroft, Twiggy
Topics: adolescence, family, friendship, parenting, work

MAID, THE

A successful Wall Street businessman poses as a maid/nanny in contemporary Paris in order to meet an eligible woman with a young daughter. To his own surprise, he does a terrific job, creating considerable trouble for his personal and professional life. This romantic comedy is an underrated joy, with terrific performances by Sheen, Bisset, and the young Shalet.

A maid-to-order romance.

1991 88m PG A-

Audience: adolescents to adults
Content: adult situations
Director: Ian Toynton
Lead Cast: Martin Sheen, Jacqueline Bisset, Victoria Shalet
Topics: family, children, parenting, work

MANHATTAN MURDER MYSTERY

When an older neighbor dies unexpectedly, an obsessive Manhattan yuppie drags her husband and friends into a search for clues to prove that the husband murdered her. A deliciously predictable, yet completely unpredictable, comedy-farce-thriller in one delightful film.

Who done what? Follow the clues!

1993 108m PG A

Audience: adolescents to adults
Content: adult themes, language
Director: Woody Allen
Lead Cast: Woody Allen, Diane Keaton, Alan Alda, Anjelica Huston, Jerry Adler
Topics: death, friendship, marriage

MAN IN THE MOON, THE

A teenage girl and her younger sister learn about love and life in the Southern U.S. during the 1950s. This bittersweet, poignant tale sensitively addresses the physical and emotional aspects of coming-of-age. It's a moving story that takes adult viewers back to their youth while giving adolescents a realistic portrait of life's hardships and joys.

An excellent but overlooked coming-of-age flick.

1991 95m PG-13 A-

Audience: mature teens to adults
Content: language, adult situations and themes, nudity
Director: Robert Mulligan
Lead Cast: Sam Waterston, Tess Harper, Gail Strickland
Topics: adolescence, death, family, friendship, romance

MANON OF THE SPRING

In this continuation of the story begun in *Jean de Florette*, a greedy French farmer and his nephew find that their spring water has stopped flowing, plunging their successful flower business into virtual bankruptcy. Some villagers conclude that God must be punishing the two, until the truth of the spring is finally made clear with significant consequences for the entire village.

Superb story of love, repentance, and forgiveness.

1987 113m PG A French (subtitled)

Audience: mature teens to adults
Content: mild language, adult themes, nudity
Director: Claude Berri
Lead Cast: Emmanuelle Béart, Yves Montand
Topics: family, religion

MAN WITHOUT A FACE, THE

A twelve-year-old misfit seeks out the town recluse for tutoring, and learns valuable lessons about "the tender mercies of injustice." Having no one else, they learn to trust each other in the face of a suspicious town. A troubling story of friendship and grace, skillfully directed by Gibson in his directorial debut, and believably acted by a versatile veteran and a refreshing newcomer.

A courageous, sensitive film.

1993 114m PG-13 A

Audience: mature teens and adults
Content: adult themes, language, intense dramatic scenes
Director: Mel Gibson
Lead Cast: Mel Gibson, Nick Stahl
Topics: adolescence, death, friendship, prejudice

MAVERICK

In this filmic knockoff of the old TV series, gambler Bret sweet-talks and connives his way into the biggest poker game of the Old West. If you like westerns and parodies, you'll enjoy the nutty characters (especially Chief Joseph), the rapid plot twists, and the comedic frontier action. Watch for a similarly fluffy—and successful—sequel.

Pappy says, "Deal it up!"

1994 127m PG A-

Audience: mature teens to adults
Content: very rough language
Director: Richard Donner
Lead Cast: Mel Gibson, Jodie Foster, James Garner,
   Graham Greene
Topics: ethics, family, friendship, prejudice

MEDICINE MAN

Dr. Campbell races against time and the destruction of the rain forest to reproduce his cancer cure. Unable to forgive himself for causing the decimation of thousands of Indians by introducing a disease into their remote forest, he devotes himself to redeeming that mistake. Frustrated, he is given new hope when an abrasive female research assistant arrives. Spectacular scenery.

An incredible quest!

1992 106m PG-13 A

Audience: teens to adults
Content: language, violence, adult themes
Director: John McTiernan
Lead Cast: Sean Connery, Lorraine Bracco
Topics: death, ethics, nature, romance, work

MEMPHIS BELLE

A crew of young flyboys battles in 1943 for survival and a chance to go home if they can complete the twenty-fifth and final mission aboard a B-17—a perilous journey into Germany. Tremendous performances, superb air-battle photography, and an inspiring story make this an outstanding true story of heroism and patriotism.

Ring the belle!

1990 104m PG-13 A- British

Audience: teens to adults
Content: language, violence
Director: Michael Caton-Jones
Lead Cast: Matthew Modine, Eric Stoltz, Tate Donovan
Topics: death, friendship, heroism, romance, war

MIGHTY DUCKS, THE

A hotshot young lawyer must coach an inept peewee hockey team as a community service sentence. In the process, he faces his own painful childhood failure that has fueled his adult need to win at all costs, and learns the value of acceptance, honesty, and teamwork. The Mighty Ducks is a warm and funny celebration of belonging, self-acceptance, and service. Catch the sequel, *D2: The Mighty Ducks*.

A terrific, underrated film.

1992 PG 100m A-

Audience: all ages
Content: mild violence, language
Director: Stephen Herek
Lead Cast: Emilio Estevez, Joss Ackland, Lane Smith
Topics: adolescence, ethics, friendship, parenting, romance, sports

MIRACLE OF THE HEART: A BOYSTOWN STORY

A troubled teen is saved from prison by the judge's offer to put him in Nebraska's Boystown. As the boy struggles with the rules and responsibilities of his new "home," the head priest faces his own conflicts with the new administrator of Boystown, who wants to change the old ways. Predictable but well-done family fare.

Another of Carney's heartwarming performances.

1986 93m NR TVM A-

Audience: all ages
Content: mild language
Director: Georg Stanford Brown
Lead Cast: Art Carney, Casey Siemaszko
Topics: adolescence, family, friendship, parenting

MISS ROSE WHITE

A young Jewish woman and her widowed father in New York City learn that her sister miraculously survived the death camps after Hitler's invasion of their Polish homeland. The arrival of the lost relative, however, sparks conflict and elicits painful memories that challenge family relationships. A superb Hallmark production.

A televisual triumph.

1992 98m PG TVM A

Audience: teens to adults
Content: adult themes, intense dramatic scenes
Director: Joseph Sargent
Lead Cast: Kyra Sedgwick, Maximilian Schell, Amanda Plummer
Topics: aging, children, death, family, marriage, religion, romance

MISSION, THE

An unlikely coalition forms between a dedicated priest and a reformed slave trader to protect a South American Indian tribe from a brutal colonial takeover. Filmed on location, the lush, breathtakingly beautiful scenery is the setting for spiritual rebirth, contrasted with intense greed and violence. This passionate and heartbreaking film is haunting in its portrayal of actual historical events of the 1750s.

Winner of Best Picture Award at Cannes.

1986 125m PG A+ British

Audience: teens to adults
Content: graphic violence, dramatic scenes, adult themes
Director: Roland Joffe
Lead Cast: Robert De Niro, Jeremy Irons, Ray McAnally, Aidan Quinn
Topics: death, ethics, friendship, heroism, nature, prejudice, religion

MISTER JOHNSON

A talented but dishonest young black man tangles with British authorities who are trying to build a road with native labor in West Africa during the 1920s. This is a fascinating look at British-African relations during England's colonial period, using the black man as a symbol of conflicting African loyalties.

Based on the novel by Joyce Cary.

1991 101m PG-13 A-

Audience: adults
Content: language, adult situations, violence
Director: Bruce Beresford
Lead Cast: Pierce Brosnan, Edward Woodward, Maynard Eziashi
Topics: marriage, prejudice, religion, work

MONKEY TROUBLE

A lonely but ingenious young girl in contemporary Los Angeles befriends a mischievous capuchin monkey trained to pick pockets and steal jewelry. While the critter's crooked owner hunts for the cute primate, the girl tries to hide her pet from parents, including her allergic step-father. Real family fare that deserves a "G" rating.

Monkey steals show!

1994 92m PG B+

Audience: all ages
Content: nothing objectionable
Director: Franco Amurri
Lead Cast: Thora Birch, Mimi Rogers, Christopher McDonald, Harvey Keitel
Topics: children, family, friendship, parenting

MOTHER'S COURAGE, A:
THE MARY THOMAS STORY

Mrs. Thomas struggles without a husband to raise all of her kids with dignity and respect in Chicago—including eventual basketball star, Isiah. Her battles with neighborhood gangs, her loving devotion to her children, and her belief in education are inspirational. A heartwarming docudrama.

A three-pointer!

1989 84m NR TVM A-

Audience: all ages
Content: mild violence
Director: John Patterson
Lead Cast: Alfre Woodard, A. J. Johnson
Topics: adolescence, family, parenting, prejudice, religion, sports, work

MRS. DOUBTFIRE

An unemployed actor hatches a clever plan to stay close to his children, who are in the custody of his estranged wife. Using his theatrical gifts, he plays the role of their nutty new nanny, "Mrs. Doubtfire." A warm, touching, and often hilarious comedy with a realistic, hopeful ending.

No doubt about it, it's hot!

1993 100m PG-13 A-

Audience: adolescents to adults
Content: adult themes, language
Director: Chris Columbus
Lead Cast: Robin Williams, Sally Field, Pierce Brosnan
Topics: family, marriage, parenting

MUCH ADO ABOUT NOTHING

Two pairs of lovers wrestle with providence, deception, wit, and evil when the men return from battle to a hospitable Italian villa. A marvelous cinematic version of Shakespeare's humorous but insightful tale about "nothing" but love—which is almost everything!

A frolicking good time!

1993 113m PG-13 A-

Audience: teens to adults
Content: adult themes, nudity
Director: Kenneth Branagh
Lead Cast: Kenneth Branagh, Emma Thompson, Keanu Reeves, Michael Keaton
Topics: friendship, romance

MUPPET CHRISTMAS CAROL, THE

Muppets "Gonzo" and "Rizzo the Rat" narrate the classic Dickens story as a live-action musical, with Michael Caine as Scrooge. It's a terrific production with superb puppetry, moving music, and humorous interludes with Gonzo and Rizzo, who inform young viewers about what will happen next and assure them that everything will turn out all right.

A future Christmas classic.

1992 98m G A

Audience: all ages
Content: intense dramatic scenes
Director: Brian Henson
Lead Cast: Michael Caine, Kermit the Frog, Miss Piggy
Topics: death, family, religion, work

MUSIC BOX, THE

A loyal daughter represents in court her kindly Hungarian immigrant father who has been accused of falsifying his citizenship papers in order to hide his identity as a former Nazi criminal. This is not courtroom high drama, but a subtle look at self-deception and human nature. Although a bit slow, the story picks up toward the end and delivers a surprising conclusion.

American film debut of German film great Mueller-Stahl.

1990 123m PG-13 B +

Audience: mature teens to adults
Content: language, adult themes
Director: Costa-Gavras
Lead Cast: Jessica Lange, Armin Mueller-Stahl, Frederic Forrest
Topics: ethics, family, war

MY FATHER'S GLORY

A companion film to Yves Robert's *My Mother's Castle*, this one focuses on the father of a turn-of-the-century French boy. As the boy matures, he recognizes his father as a talented educator and a loving father, but also as a man with the need to prove himself before other men. Based on the reminiscences of Marcel Pagnol.

Endearing story about childhood and family life.

1991 110m G A French (subtitled)

Audience: all ages
Content: mild language
Director: Yves Robert
Lead Cast: Philippe Caubert, Nathalie Roussel, Didier Pain
Topics: children, family, marriage, parenting, work

MY GIRL 2

On the brink of womanhood, Vada (a bright adolescent living with her mortician father and pregnant stepmother) goes to California in search of her identity. Her goal is to find out all she can about her mother, who died when she was a baby. Along the way, Vada's goodness rubs off on everyone. Generally an upbeat, sweet, and delightful film.

Skip *My Girl*, but don't miss this sweet sequel!

1994 99m PG A-

Audience: school-age to adults
Content: adult themes, language
Director: Howard Zieff
Lead Cast: Anna Chlumsky, Austin O'Brien, Dan Aykroyd, Jamie Lee Curtis, Richard Masur
Topics: adolescence, death, friendship, marriage, romance

MY MOTHER'S CASTLE

A grown man recalls the summers during the turn of the century in southern France at a cottage his mother loved. Based on the remembrances of Marcel Pagnol, the film marvelously captures the mother's loving sensitivity and the family's annual renewal at the summer home. In order to get to the cottage for relaxed weekends, the family had to sneak through private estates. Also see *My Father's Glory*.

Profoundly satisfying tale about motherhood.

1991 98m G A French (subtitled)

Audience: all ages
Content: mild language
Director: Yves Robert
Lead Cast: Philippe Caubert, Nathalie Roussel, Didier Pain
Topics: children, family, marriage, nature, parenting

MY NAME IS BILL W.

He soared to the top of Wall Street on an alcoholic high, then crashed to the bottom when he couldn't control his drinking. As hard as he tried, he couldn't stay sober until he found strength in the honesty and understanding of fellow drunks. A stirring account (Emmy for Woods) of the founding of Alcoholics Anonymous by Bill Wilson and Dr. Robert Smith.

Take the first step . . .

1989 100m NR TVM B+

Audience: adolescents to adults
Content: mild violence, language, intense dramatic scenes
Director: Daniel Petrie
Lead Cast: James Woods, James Garner, JoBeth Williams, Gary Sinese
Topics: disability, friendship, marriage

NECESSARY PARTIES

When a fifteen-year-old boy's parents announce plans to divorce, he decides to fight it in court, holding the family together for himself and his younger sister. This sensitive treatment of the trauma of family breakup is based on Barbara Dana's book. Arkin is outstanding as the eccentric lawyer turned auto mechanic.

The verdict is in—a winner!

1988 109m NR TVM A

Audience: adolescents to adults
Content: language
Director: Gwen Arner
Lead Cast: Alan Arkin, Mark Paul Gosselaar, Barbara Dana
Topics: adolescence, family, marriage

NEWSIES

When publishing magnate Joseph Pulitzer unfairly raises the pick-up price of papers for newsboys, one of them organizes a strike. The newsies face poverty and violence when they strike, but they stand together under pressure. Although the music is disappointing, the dancing makes up for it in this stagy musical nicely set in turn-of-the-century America.

Good news!

1992 120m PG B +

Audience: adolescents to adults
Content: language, violence, intense dramatic scenes
Director: Kenny Ortega
Lead Cast: Christian Bale, David Moscow, Robert Duvall
Topics: adolescence, ethics, family, friendship, heroism, romance, work

NOT WITHOUT MY DAUGHTER

A young American mother and her daughter are held "hostage" in Iran by her native husband after the Islamic revolution deposes the Shah and eliminates a married woman's rights. This heartwrenching tale is superbly performed by Field and Molina, who nicely captures the father's own ambivalence about the benefits of the revolution. Based on Betty Mahmoody's book.

A heroic mother.

1991 111m PG-13 A

Audience: teens to adults
Content: violence, adult themes
Director: Brian Gilbert
Lead Cast: Sally Field, Alfred Molina, Sheila Rosenthal
Topics: children, heroism, family, marriage, prejudice, religion

OF MICE AND MEN

A mismatched pair of bindle stiffs finds work on a ranch during the Depression until the mentally impaired one lands in "very bad" trouble. They dream that someday they'll have their own place, but the harsh realities of their circumstances prevent realization of that dream. A remarkable version of John Steinbeck's heartwrenching classic of friendship.

A strong and tender tragedy.

1992 110m PG-13 A

Audience: teens to adults
Content: violence, language, adult themes
Director: Gary Sinise
Lead Cast: John Malkovich, Gary Sinise, Ray Walston
Topics: disability, friendship, prejudice, work

OLIVER AND COMPANY

In this animated Disney variation on the story of Oliver Twist, the orphaned kitten, Oliver, is befriended by a dog, Dodger, and a human, Fagin. Oliver runs with the canine pack of thieves until he is adopted by a little girl. The story departs from the original further as Oliver and his canine friends team up to rescue the girl from a mobster. Great characterizations and toe-tapping music.

Good company!

1988 72m G A Animated

Audience: all ages
Content: intense dramatic scenes
Director: George Scribner
Lead Cast: (voices) Bette Midler, Billy Joel, Cheech Marin, Joey Lawrence
Topics: friendship, heroism

OLLIE HOPNOODLE'S HAVEN OF BLISS

Lovers of Jean Shepherd's antinostalgic feature film, *A Christmas Story* (see Classic Videos), will surely enjoy this similarly wacky TV movie. Adolescent Ralphie learns the truth about work and vacations. His family travels to Michigan on rural roads, suffering all of the "joyful" mishaps that make up the treasured tales of such memorable family trips.

A chronicle of craziness.

1993 87m NR TVM A-

Audience: adolescents to adults
Content: language
Director: Dick Bartlett
Lead Cast: Jerry O'Connell, James B. Sikking, Dorothy Lyman
Topics: adolescence, family, work

ONE AGAINST THE WIND

A British countess living in Paris during WW II impulsively rescues an RAF pilot and begins an operation of smuggling Allied soldiers to safety under the noses of the Nazis. Based on the true story of the indomitable Mary Lindell, who was twice decorated for bravery, it is a riveting account of the French underground.

Stunning and courageous.

1991 96m PG A- U.S./Luxembourg

Audience: teens to adults
Content: language, violence
Director: Larry Elikann
Lead Cast: Judy Davis, Sam Neill, Denholm Elliott
Topics: heroism, romance, war

ONE MORE MOUNTAIN

A wealthy family from Illinois travels by wagon train with the infamous Donner party to California. They encounter starvation, ostracism, and the harshest winter storms in history after they separate from the Donner group. This realistic portrayal of hardship doesn't glamorize pioneer life, but draws the viewer in to appreciate the courage and strength of these people.

Not just another prairie ride.

1994 95m NR TVM A

Audience: adolescents to adults
Content: mild violence, intense dramatic scenes
Director: Dick Lowry
Lead Cast: Meredith Baxter, Chris Cooper, Larry Drake, Robert Duncan McNeill, Laurie O'Brien
Topics: death, family, heroism, nature, prejudice

O PIONEERS!

At the turn of the century, an independent young woman turns the family's struggling farm into a wealthy estate through courage, fairness, and kindness. Though the harsh Nebraska prairie becomes her beloved home, it can't fully replace her love for an old friend who left as a teenager. This tale of perseverance is an accurate and enjoyable adaptation of the Willa Cather novel.

O K!

1992 99m NR TVM A

Audience: adolescents to adults
Content: mild violence, adult themes
Director: Glenn Jordan
Lead Cast: Jessica Lange, David Strathairn
Topics: aging, family, friendship, romance, work

OSCAR

When Chicago's biggest gangster promises his dying father he'll go straight, he discovers it's harder than a life of crime. This hilarious spoof of gangster movies is fast-paced fun, complete with mistaken identities, mismatched lovers, misplaced black bags, and plenty of mischief. Stallone is surprisingly funny in the midst of an array of oddballs.

No "Oscar," but great fun.

1991 109m PG B +

Audience: adolescents to adults
Content: language, adult themes
Director: John Landis
Lead Cast: Sylvester Stallone, Ornella Muti, Marisa Tomei
Topics: ethics, family, marriage, romance

OUTSIDE CHANCE OF MAXIMILIAN GLICK, THE

Max is about to be bar mitzvahed in 1960 in a small town in western Canada, but he has last-minute doubts when his parents won't let him perform with a Gentile in a piano competition. This charming film captures both the innocence of childhood and the adult complexities of living in a multicultural society.

Shalom!

1988 95m G A- Canadian

Audience: all ages
Content: adult themes
Director: Allan A. Goldstein
Lead Cast: Saul Rubinek, Jan Rubes
Topics: adolescence, family, friendship, parenting, religion, romance

OX, THE

In mid-19th-century Sweden, a poor, desperate farmworker kills his employer's ox one winter to save his wife and young daughter from starvation. Filled with guilt and fear, he and his spouse try to maintain normal relationships in the small, highly religious community. This powerful film addresses the certainty of human sin and the joy of human forgiveness.

A moving tale.

1992 90m NR A Swedish (subtitled)

Audience: adults
Content: adult situations and themes
Director: Sven Nykvist
Lead Cast: Stellan Skarsgard, Ewa Froling, Liv Ullmann, Max von Sydow
Topics: death, ethics, marriage, parenting, religion, work

PARADISE

A small-town Southern couple, estranged by a tragedy, shepherds a young boy who comes to visit for the summer. As the boy and a neighborhood girl learn about life together, the couple reevaluates its own relationship. There are many tender moments in this fine film, although it starts out a bit slowly.

Warm tale of reborn relationships.

1991 108m PG-13 B+

Audience: mature teens to adults
Content: language, adult situations, nudity
Director: Mary Agnes Donoghue
Lead Cast: Melanie Griffith, Don Johnson, Elijah Wood
Topics: children, family, friendship, marriage

PELLE THE CONQUEROR

An aging Swedish widower and his young son travel to Denmark late in the 19th century in hopes of a better life. They take the only work they can get on a farm, but they continue to dream of a home, family, and respect in spite of repeated setbacks. A deeply moving, sometimes disturbing story that never completely gives up hope in the face of repeated trials and tribulations.

Academy Award for best foreign film.

1988 149m PG-13 A- Danish/Swedish (dubbed)

Audience: adults
Content: language, adult situations
Director: Bille August
Lead Cast: Max von Sydow, Pelle Hvenegaard
Topics: adolescence, marriage, parenting, prejudice, work

PERFECT HARMONY

The status quo of an exclusive Southern boys' school is threatened by the arrival of the new music teacher and the growing friendship between one of the students and a local black boy. A mutual love of music enables them to look past their differences. Their mutual respect gives them the courage to face hatred and prejudice and to stand up for justice.

Sings with courage.

1991 95m NR TVM A-

Audience: school-age to adults
Content: mild violence
Director: Will Mackenzie
Lead Cast: Peter Scolari, Darrin McGavin, Moses Gunn
Topics: adolescence, ethics, family, friendship, prejudice

PISTOL, THE: THE BIRTH OF A LEGEND

This family-oriented historical drama follows the life of basketball legend "Pistol" Pete Maravich, whose relationship with his father was crucial in his success on and off the courts. Young Pete learns that determination and self-confidence require hope and faith as he overcomes his own doubts to become a champion of the game. True family fare.

Give it a shot.

1990 95m G A-

Audience: all ages
Content: nothing objectionable
Director: Frank C. Schroeder
Lead Cast: Millie Perkins, Nick Benedict, Adam Guier
Topics: adolescence, family, friendship, parenting, sports

PRANCER

A nine-year-old girl finds a wounded reindeer in the woods and, believing it to be Santa's "Prancer," nurses it back to health so it can return to Claus. Her efforts affect cynical and troubled adults, who need a bit more "faith" in their lives. Although predictable, this family movie is charming and uplifting any time of year.

An "endeering" film.

1989 96m G B+

Audience: all ages
Content: nothing objectionable
Director: John Hancock
Lead Cast: Sam Elliott, Rebecca Harrell, Cloris Leachman
Topics: children, friendship, parenting

PRETTY IN PINK

A self-reliant girl from the wrong side of the tracks is put off guard when one of the "richies" shows interest. Ringwald is laudable as a strong, principled, but not perfect teen able to face down peer pressure. Some of the language will cause parents to cringe, but it only reinforces the contrast between the shallow lives of most of the teens and Andy's strength and tenderness.

Pretty good teen flick.

1986 96m PG-13 B+

Audience: mature teens to adults
Content: language, adult themes
Director: Howard Deutch
Lead Cast: Molly Ringwald, Jon Cryer, Andrew McCarthy, Annie Potts, Harry Dean Stanton
Topics: adolescence, family, friendship, prejudice, romance

PRINCE CASPIAN and THE VOYAGE OF THE DAWN TREADER (THE CHRONICLES OF NARNIA)

In the second of C. S. Lewis's *Chronicles of Narnia*, young Prince Caspian calls on the four children to help him defeat wicked King Miraz and to restore Narnia to its former glory. Caspian sails in search of seven lords who have been banished by Miraz, encountering strange adventures with Lucy, Edmund, and their obnoxious cousin, Eustace, on their journey to the eastern edge of the world. WonderWorks.

Take the voyage into another world.

1988 165m NR TVM B+

Audience: school-age to adults
Content: mild violence
Director: Alex Kirby
Lead Cast: Richard Dempsey, Sophie Cook, Jonathan Scott, Sophie Wilcox
Topics: death, friendship, heroism, religion, war

PRINCESS BRIDE, THE

A beautiful young woman is kidnapped to marry an unwanted suitor after believing her true love to be dead. This adventure is pure fantasy for young viewers, while adults will also enjoy the imaginative, subtly humorous twists. Full of swordplay and perilous wizardry, it also does "have a lot of kissing in it."

Tongue-in-cheek fantasy.

1987 98m PG A-

Audience: school-age to adults
Content: mild violence, language
Director: Rob Reiner
Lead Cast: Cary Elwes, Robin Wright, Mandy Patinkin, Chris Sarandon, Andre the Giant, Wallace Shawn, Billy Crystal, Carol Kane, Peter Falk, Fred Savage
Topics: death, heroism, romance

PROJECT X

A mischievous young Air Force pilot discovers that the chimps he is caring for in a top-secret project are being used for harmful military experiments on a base in Florida. He has to decide which is more important, his own military career or the life of a clever, affectionate chimp. A remarkably believable tale about animal abuse that also packs quite a few laughs.

Go bananas!

1987 106m PG B+

Audience: adolescents to adults
Content: language, intense dramatic scenes
Director: Jonathan Kaplan
Lead Cast: Matthew Broderick, Jonathan Kaplan, Helen Hunt
Topics: ethics, friendship, work

QUIGLEY DOWN UNDER

A Yank sharpshooter learns his new Australian boss wants his skills not for shooting dingos, but for killing Aborigines. In the tradition of the best old westerns, this film takes us to the "new West," where money and power equal right. But Selleck, as Quigley, uses his strength and skill to stand up for the powerless. San Giacomo is delightful as "Crazy Cora."

High adventure in the new West.

1990 121m PG-13 A-

Audience: mature teens and adults
Content: language, violence, adult themes
Director: Simon Wincer
Lead Cast: Tom Selleck, Laura San Giacomo, Alan Rickman
Topics: ethics, heroism, prejudice, romance

RACE TO FREEDOM—
THE UNDERGROUND RAILROAD

Four young slaves encounter hardship and treachery when they flee their master with the help of the Underground Railroad. Inspired by Barbara Smucker's novel, *Underground to Canada*, this Hallmark Hall of Fame film stirringly portrays the desperation and courage of the runaways and those who risked their lives to help them reach freedom.

Hop on board the rails!

1994 98m NR TVM A Canadian

Audience: mature teens to adults
Content: violence, intense dramatic scenes
Director: Don McBrearty
Lead Cast: Janet Bailey, Courtney B. Vance, Michael Riley, Ron White, Dawnn Lewis, Glynn Turman
Topics: ethics, heroism, prejudice

RADICALS, THE

Two devout young adults in 16th-century Europe leave their religious orders in search of authentic faith and become early martyrs in the birth of the Anabaptist movement. Based on the true story of the Sattlers, this film is a touching chronicle of the radical group that disavowed both Catholics and Protestants in its dedication to live life in complete surrender to God.

Radical faith, stunningly portrayed.

1989 99m NR B

Audience: teens to adults
Content: intense dramatic scenes
Director: Paul V. Carrera
Lead Cast: Norbert Weisser, Leigh Lombardi, Mark Lenard
Topics: prejudice, religion, romance, war

RADIO DAYS

Woody Allen's satirical look at pretelevision days highlights the way Americans' dreams were woven out of the tapestry of deceptive popular culture. An adolescent boy in Brooklyn in the 1940s finds that radio's dreamy views of life contrast starkly with his own family's trials and tribulations. Weak on plot, but very strong on anti-nostalgic vignettes of the way things really were.

The not-so-good old days.

1987 85m PG A-

Audience: adolescents to adults
Content: adult situations and themes, language
Director: Woody Allen
Lead Cast: Mia Farrow, Dianne Wiest, Seth Green, Michael Tucker
Topics: adolescence, children, family, parenting, romance, work

RAISE THE RED LANTERN

A beautiful young woman in rural China during the 1920s has to quit the university when her father dies, and she becomes the fourth "mistress" in the harem at a nobleman's palatial estate. Her hopes for a happy life are quickly dashed, however, as she discovers a cold, cruel world of jealousy, deception, and revenge. A moving portrait of how tradition can institutionalize evil.

A cinematic triumph.

1991 122m PG A China/Taiwan/Hong Kong

Audience: adults
Content: adult situations and themes
Director: Zhang Yimou
Lead Cast: Gong Li, Ma Jingwu, He Caifei
Topics: friendship, marriage

RAISIN IN THE SUN, A

This is a superb television production of Lorraine Hansberry's play about a black family living in an all-white neighborhood in Chicago. By examining the joys and tribulations of family, the story reveals much about the human condition as well as about racism in America. Critically acclaimed production by American Playhouse.

A classic.

1988 168m NR TVM A

Audience: adolescents to adults
Content: adult situations and themes
Director: Bill Duke
Lead Cast: Danny Glover, Esther Rolle, Starletta Dupois
Topics: adolescence, children, family, friendship, marriage, parenting, prejudice

REGARDING HENRY

A wealthy and highly esteemed attorney is shot almost fatally by a gunman robbing a small store in Manhattan. Suddenly the attorney is faced not only with his own mortality, but also with his weaknesses as a husband and father. The result is an inspiring tale about the rebirth of a yuppie who decides to put love and family ahead of greed and profession.

Regarding love and life.

1991 100m PG-13 A-

Audience: adolescents to adults
Content: language
Director: Mike Nichols
Lead Cast: Harrison Ford, Annette Bening, Bill Nunn
Topics: disability, ethics, family, friendship, marriage, parenting, work

REMAINS OF THE DAY, THE

The head butler and housekeeper in an English estate deal with conflicting loyalties and passions as WW II threatens. This superbly crafted film, shot in Super 35, creates a powerful portrait of unrequited love and suppressed conscience. One of Hopkins's best performances—a tour de force.

For a special day!

1993 132m PG A

Audience: teens to adults
Content: adult themes
Director: James Ivory
Lead Cast: Anthony Hopkins, Emma Thompson, James Fox, Christopher Reeve
Topics: aging, ethics, friendship, romance, work

RESCUERS DOWN UNDER, THE

Two fearless mice from the Rescue Aid Society travel to Australia to help a young boy protect a rare golden eagle against an evil poacher. Full of high adventure, this animated sequel to *The Rescuers* has enough suspense without terrifying younger viewers. Disney throws in a little romance and hilarity for a delightful film.

Go "down under" and come up laughing.

1990 74m G B+ Animated

Audience: all ages
Content: nothing objectionable
Director: Hendel Butoy
Lead Cast: (voices) Bob Newhart, Eva Gabor, John Candy, George C. Scott
Topics: ethics, friendship, heroism, nature, romance

RETURN TO SNOWY RIVER

The man from Snowy River returns to Snowy River and his love, but finds that even with his 100 horses and modest home he still must earn the respect of her powerful father in order to win her from a planned marriage to another man. He must also deal with a feud between local landowners. This is another fast-paced adventure with splendid photography of Australia's spectacular Victoria Alps.

Breathtaking return.

1988 98m PG A Australian

Audience: adolescents to adults
Content: violence, language, adult themes
Director: Geoff Burrowes
Lead Cast: Tom Burlinson, Sigrid Thornton, Brian Dennehy
Topics: ethics, family, friendship, heroism, prejudice, romance

RISE AND WALK: THE DENNIS BYRD STORY

When a freak football injury leaves him paralyzed, Dennis Byrd refuses to believe that he will never walk again, depending on his wife, his therapist, and his faith in God to make a miracle. In the same vein as *Brian's Song*, *Rise and Walk* is a feel-good movie about an admirable man.

Cheer this one on!

1994 96m NR TVM B

Audience: adolescents to adults
Content: intense dramatic scenes
Director: Michael Dinner
Lead Cast: Peter Berg, Kathy Morris, Johann Carlo
Topics: disability, friendship, religion, sports

RIVER RUNS THROUGH IT, A

Two very different brothers grow up together in eastern Montana during the 1920s and 1930s, pursuing divergent careers, relationships, and lifestyles. One is worldly and independent, the other refined and flexible. Only the Big Blackfoot River brings them and their stern father, a Presbyterian minister, together for the common ritual of fly-fishing. Based on Norman Maclean's autobiographical novella.

Nominated for three Academy Awards.

1992 123m PG-13 A-

Audience: adults
Content: very rough language, adult situations and themes, nudity
Director: Robert Redford
Lead Cast: Craig Sheffer, Brad Pitt, Tom Skerritt
Topics: adolescence, death, family, friendship, nature, prejudice, romance

ROCKETEER, THE

A young stunt pilot and his inventive partner in 1938 stumble upon an experimental rocket pack that enables individuals to fly. Meanwhile, federal agents and the mob are searching for the rocket pack, and the aeronautical duo is caught in an international struggle for control of the technology. With the fabulous special effects and the pilot's growing romance, it's a great, underrated movie.

Blast off!

1991 110m PG A-

Audience: adolescents to adults
Content: mild language, violence
Director: Joe Johnston
Lead Cast: William O. Campbell, Jennifer Connelly, Alan Arkin
Topics: heroism, romance, war

ROMERO

This well-made film tells the story of El Salvador's Archbishop Oscar Romero, who was killed in 1980, presumably by a government-supported death squad, for his growing support of economic reform and Indian rights. Produced by the Paulists, this film compellingly captures the tensions within the church as well as the escalating conflict in Central America.

A moving tribute.

1989 101m PG-13 A

Audience: mature teens to adults
Content: graphic violence, adult situations, intense dramatic scenes, nudity
Director: John Duigan
Lead Cast: Raul Julia, Richard Jordan, Ana Alicia, Eddie Velez
Topics: death, ethics, heroism, prejudice, religion

ROOKIE OF THE YEAR

A clumsy twelve-year-old's dream comes true when his broken arm heals so well that the Chicago Cubs sign him as their starting pitcher. This refreshing comedy presents a totally likable adolescent whose fame doesn't get in the way of friendship, good sense, respect, and love.

A terrific family comedy.

1993 115m PG A-

Audience: school-age to adults
Content: mild language
Director: Daniel Stern
Lead Cast: Thomas Ian Nicholas, Gary Busey, Dan Hedaya
Topics: adolescence, family, friendship, romance, sports

ROSE GARDEN, THE

In contemporary Germany, a female attorney tries to defend a Jewish victim of the Nazi concentration camps who attacks a former officer of the Third Reich. Along the way she discovers much about atrocities committed by Nazis against Jewish children, changing her relationship with her own daughter and estranged husband. A powerful drama about inhumanity, justice, and love.

Best actress Golden Globe nominee.

1989 109m PG-13 B +

Audience: adults
Content: adult situations and themes
Director: Fons Rademakers
Lead Cast: Liv Ullmann, Maximilian Schell, Peter Fonda
Topics: ethics, marriage, parenting, prejudice, war

RUDY

A diminutive teen from a working-class family pursues his impossible goal to play football for Notre Dame against all odds and with no encouragement. Rudy's tenacity is admirable, but almost painful to watch. It's refreshing to see someone succeed using every available ethical means! Based on a true story.

An inspiration to all underdogs!

1993 110m PG-13 A-

Audience: teens to adults
Content: language
Director: David Anspaugh
Lead Cast: Sean Astin, Ned Beatty, Charles S. Dutton, Jason Miller, Lili Taylor, Robert Prosky
Topics: friendship, religion, sports

RUNNING ON EMPTY

Two radical antiwar activists are forced to raise their children on the road for years as they avoid detection by the FBI, which seeks them for blowing up a napalm lab and injuring a worker. When their adolescent son begins thinking about romance and college, the couple must face the past. Compellingly addresses the need for a strong family life, a stable identity, and generational continuity.

An emotionally full drama.

1988 114m PG-13 A-

Audience: mature teens to adults
Content: very rough language
Director: Sidney Lumet
Lead Cast: Christine Lahti, Judd Hirsch, Martha Plimpton, River Phoenix
Topics: adolescence, ethics, family, friendship, parenting, romance

SAND FAIRY, THE

A "Psammead," or sand fairy, who grants wishes sends four children on daily adventures according to their wish, but the wishes never turn out the way they expect. A delightful story based on E. Nesbit's book, *Five Children and It* (the fifth is a baby brother), that teaches a valuable lesson about contentment.

Wishing can be dangerous!

1991 139m NR B+ British

Audience: school-age to adults
Content: nothing objectionable
Director: Richard Callanan
Lead Cast: Simon Godwin, Nicole Mowat, Charlie Richards, Tamzen Audas, Laura Brattan
Topics: children, ethics

SANDLOT, THE

A fifth-grade boy in the 1960s moves to a new neighborhood with his mother and stepfather, befriending the local boys who live all summer for sandlot baseball. Their adventures include coeds at the swimming pool, chewing tobacco at the carnival, and "the beast" who ferociously defends one of the neighboring yards of legend. A nostalgic period movie with humorous and touching scenes.

A home-run movie.

1993 108m PG A-

Audience: adolescents to adults
Content: language, intense dramatic scenes
Director: David Mickey Evans
Lead Cast: Mike Vitar, Tom Guiry
Topics: adolescence, friendship, parenting, sports

SARAFINA!

A teenage schoolgirl is caught up in the youth rebellion against apartheid in South Africa, but the wise words of her teacher help her to reject violence as the road to freedom. Confusing at times due to its adaptation from a stage musical, but a hopeful, if not happy, ending.

A moving appeal for justice.

1992 96m PG-13 B+ U.S./British/French

Audience: mature teens to adults
Content: graphic violence, language, intense dramatic scenes
Director: Darrell James Roodt
Lead Cast: Leleti Khumalo, Whoopi Goldberg, Miriam Makeba, John Kani, Mbongeni Ngema
Topics: death, ethics, family, friendship, heroism, prejudice, war

SARAH, PLAIN AND TALL

A widowed Kansas farmer needs help raising his two children, but he gets more than he bargained for when a strong-willed New Englander responds to his ad for a mail-order bride. Sarah is not only "plain and tall," but forthright, generous, and stubborn. Gradually her gentle nurturing eases the children's pain over the loss of their mother, but the father must come to terms with his painful loss before he can accept a new life and love. Followed by *Skylark*.

Superb Hallmark production.

1990 98m NR TVM A

Audience: all ages
Content: intense dramatic scenes
Director: Glenn Jordan
Lead Cast: Glenn Close, Christopher Walken, Lexi Randall
Topics: death, family, friendship, marriage, nature, romance, work

SAY ANYTHING . . .

A laid-back high schooler persuades the class valedictorian to go out with him, and love blossoms. This refreshingly original teen pic is sensitive and believable. The characters are likable and their struggles are handled compassionately. Although casual sex is portrayed as acceptable, the other messages include honesty, self-sacrifice, and commitment.

Say "yes" to this quality teen flick.

1989 100m PG-13 A

Audience: teens to adults
Content: language, adult themes
Director: Cameron Crowe
Lead Cast: John Cusack, Ione Skye, John Mahoney
Topics: adolescence, ethics, family, friendship, parenting, prejudice, romance

SEARCHING FOR BOBBY FISCHER

In this delightfully unusual film, a seven-year-old chess prodigy and his driven father in New York City learn about the game and about life from two very different mentors, a professional chess instructor and a streetwise speed-chess hustler. A subtle, superbly directed movie, based on the nonfiction book by the father, Fred Waitzkin.

Check this one out!

1993 105m PG A

Audience: adolescents to adults
Content: nothing objectionable
Director: Steven Zaillian
Lead Cast: Joe Montegna, Joan Allen, Max Pomeranc, Ben Kingsley
Topics: children, family, friendship, parenting

SECRET GARDEN, THE

When a young British girl's parents suddenly die in India, she is sent home to the palatial estate of a despondent family member. There she discovers a secret garden, an unexpected playmate, and a mysterious invalid boy. Together they courageously overcome fears as they transform the garden into a symbol of hope and a place of beauty. Hallmark production based on Frances Hodgson Burnett's novel.

Plant the tape in your VCR.

1992 99m PG TVM A

Audience: all ages
Content: nothing objectionable
Director: Alan Grint
Lead Cast: Gennie James, Barret Oliver, Jadrien Steele
Topics: adolescence, death, disability, family, friendship, parenting, romance

SECRET GARDEN, THE

When a spoiled but unloved orphan is taken in by her reclusive uncle in his dark, mysterious manor, her bitter heart is renewed by unexpected friendship and the discovery of a secret garden. This version of the beloved story by Frances Hodgson Burnett is lavishly filmed. The acting of the young stars is remarkable. The dark despair in the first part of the film contrasts sharply with the vibrant rebirth of the garden and the manor's inhabitants in the end.

A stunning portrayal of rebirth.

1993 100m G A

Audience: adolescents to adults
Content: nothing objectionable
Director: Agnieszka Holland
Lead Cast: Maggie Smith, Kate Maberly, Heydon Prowse, Andrew Knott
Topics: children, death, family, friendship, nature, parenting

SEE YOU IN THE MORNING

A newly divorced man and a recently widowed woman face the struggle of molding a new family with her two children. The step-dad sensitively enters the new family, making a few mistakes but hopefully moving ahead. This film deals insightfully and gently with the problems of family breakup and the blending of new families.

This flick will brighten your day.

1989 119m PG-13 A-

Audience: teens to adults
Content: adult situations
Director: Alan J. Pakula
Lead Cast: Jeff Bridges, Alice Krige, Farrah Fawcett
Topics: children, death, family, marriage, parenting, romance

SHADOWLANDS

This historical drama movingly traces the unusual romance and marriage in the 1950s between popular Christian author, C. S. Lewis, and a divorced American woman. The photography and script are excellent, although the semi-tragic ending seems to dispute Lewis's own writings during the later years of his life. Also see *C. S. Lewis Through the Shadowlands* (Classic Videos).

Surprised by joy!

1993 127m PG A-

Audience: teens to adults
Content: adult themes
Director: Richard Attenborough
Lead Cast: Anthony Hopkins, Debra Winger
Topics: death, friendship, marriage, religion, romance

SHELL SEEKERS, THE

After suffering a heart attack, a woman journeys back to her childhood in search of the joy she once knew, embodied in a painting her father had done of her with her mother. When she shares with others her love of simple, priceless treasures, she discovers herself in a new way. Based on the novel by Rosamunde Pilcher.

Worth finding!

1993 94m PG A- U.S./British

Audience: teens to adults
Content: adult themes
Director: Waris Hussein
Lead Cast: Angela Lansbury, Sam Wanamaker, Irene Worth, Christopher Bowen, Michael Gough, Patricia Hodge, Denis Quilley, Sophie Ward
Topics: family, parenting, romance

SHIPWRECKED

A young ship's boy sails into adventures, discovering dark secrets, pirates' treasure, true friends, and courage. A wonderful Disney presentation for everyone who loves high-seas adventure. It combines romance with comedy and action. Several comedic twists add lightness to the fine adventure yarn.

Set sail with this one.

1990 93m PG A Norwegian

Audience: school-age to adults
Content: violence
Director: Nils Gaup
Lead Cast: Stian Smestad, Gabriel Byrne, Louisa Haigh
Topics: adolescence, death, family, friendship, heroism

SHORT CIRCUIT

A robot created for military purposes is struck by lightning and takes on human qualities. After he escapes the lab, the race is on to find him. His inventors hope to save him, while the military is on a seek-and-destroy mission. Meanwhile, the robot is hiding out with a beautiful animal lover who thinks the robot is an alien. Delightful romantic comedy with a dash of adventure.

Plug in for fun.

1986 99m PG B

Audience: school-age to adults
Content: language, mild violence
Director: John Badham
Lead Cast: Steve Guttenberg, Ally Sheedy, Fisher Stevens
Topics: ethics, friendship, romance, work

SHORT CIRCUIT II

In the sequel to *Short Circuit*, the robot develops superhuman intelligence and a desire to fit in with the popular culture of the city. Between the robot's misinterpretations and his human friend's malaprops, the film generates enough humorous confusion to please just about any viewer. One of the few cases of the sequel being better than the original.

Even more juice!

1988 112m PG B +

Audience: school-age to adults
Content: language, mild violence
Director: Kenneth Johnson
Lead Cast: Fisher Stevens, Michael McKean, Cynthia Gibb
Topics: ethics, friendship, heroism, romance, work

SIDE BY SIDE

When three lifelong friends are forced to retire, they combine their talents to begin a clothing company that caters to seniors. The years have tempered the humor of these three stars, and the story is gently humorous and touching. This TV flick addresses age discrimination and reveals the multidimensional nature of seniors.

Seasoned talent.

1988 100m NR TVM A-

Audience: adolescents to adults
Content: language, adult themes
Director: Jack Bender
Lead Cast: Milton Berle, Sid Caesar, Danny Thomas
Topics: aging, friendship, romance, work

SIDEKICKS

An asthmatic underdog fantasizes about fighting injustice at the side of his hero, Chuck Norris. When he begins training in the martial arts, his fantasy comes true. Soon he learns about self-confidence, discipline, and teamwork. May be too violent for some younger viewers.

A kick for martial arts enthusiasts.

1993 100m PG B

Audience: adolescents to adults
Content: mild violence, language
Director: Aaron Norris
Lead Cast: Jonathan Brandis, Mako, Chuck Norris, Beau Bridges, Joe Piscopo, Julia Nickson-Soul, Danica McKellar
Topics: adolescence, heroism, prejudice, sports

SILVER CHAIR, THE
(THE CHRONICLES OF NARNIA)

Eustace is summoned back to Narnia with his friend Jill to find Caspian's kidnapped son, Rilian. They must follow the four signs given by Aslan in order to complete this mission. Though their journey is dangerous, they are accompanied by an eccentric creature who keeps their spirits up in spite of his dire predictions. Concludes the WonderWorks presentation of *The Chronicles of Narnia*.

Enchanting!

1988 165m NR TVM B +

Audience: school-age to adults
Content: mild violence
Director: Alex Kirby
Lead Cast: David Thwaites, Camilla Power, Richard Henders, Tom Baker
Topics: adolescence, friendship, heroism, religion

SILVER STALLION: KING OF THE WILD BRUMBIES, THE

Her mother's story of a beautiful wild stallion comes to life for a sensitive girl of the Australian highlands. This is a magnificently filmed portrait of the wild and exquisite high country, set to a haunting score. A horse lover's delight—with a shocking finale—based on the book *The Silver Brumby* by Elyne Mitchell.

Majestic!

1993 93m G A- Australian

Audience: school-age to adult
Content: intense dramatic scenes
Director: John Tatoulis
Lead Cast: Caroline Goodall, Russell Crowe, Ami Daemion
Topics: friendship, heroism, nature

SISTER ACT

A lounge singer wannabe witnesses a murder and is cloistered by police in a dying convent for protection. She starts a swingin' gospel choir and rejuvenates Sunday worship at the inner-city parish. This is a warm and funny comedy with some terrific music which borders on being irreligious, but is all in good fun.

Don't miss this act.

1992 100m PG A

Audience: adolescents to adults
Content: language, mild violence, adult themes
Director: Emile Ardolino
Lead Cast: Whoopi Goldberg, Maggie Smith, Kathy Najimy
Topics: ethics, friendship, religion

SISTER ACT II: BACK IN THE HABIT

The former nightclub singer (from *Sister Act*) goes back "undercover" as Sister Mary Clarence to help the nuns turn their school and their students around. With her radical methods, Mary Clarence wins over the students and works them into shape for the state music competition. Delightful and energetic, with more fantastic music bursting with soul!

A joyful reprise!

1993 120m PG A

Audience: school-age to adults
Content: language
Director: Bill Duke
Lead Cast: Whoopi Goldberg, Kathy Najimy, Mary Wickes, Wendy Makkena, Maggie Smith
Topics: adolescence, friendship, religion

SKYLARK

In the midst of a severe Kansas drought, a family works together to save its farm from the ruin facing the entire community. As the crop fails, the well dries up, and fire destroys the barn, they must separate to survive. While the mother takes the children for a delightful visit to her beloved Maine coast, the father stays behind to keep the farm going. Sequel to *Sarah, Plain and Tall*.

Another excellent Hallmark presentation.

1993 97m NR A

Audience: all ages
Content: nothing objectionable
Director: Joseph Sargent
Lead Cast: Glenn Close, Christopher Walken, Lexi Randall
Topics: family, friendship, marriage, nature, work

SLEEPLESS IN SEATTLE

A lonely young widower in Seattle and an unhappily engaged woman in Baltimore are magically brought together by a radio call-in show and the precocious antics of the widower's son. This is a totally predictable tearjerker that makes fun of romantic comedies while simultaneously becoming one.

Stay up to see it.

1993 101m PG A-

Audience: all ages
Content: adult themes
Director: Nora Ephron, Rob Reiner
Lead Cast: Tom Hanks, Meg Ryan
Topics: adolescence, death, marriage, parenting, romance

SNEAKERS

An offbeat and eccentric group of computer-hacking security consultants tackles the biggest case of their lives—tracking down the "black box" that permits owners to break the codes of all major governmental and financial data systems in the U.S. A terrific cast and plenty of suspense make this a fun movie, even if the plot more than stretches reality.

Mission, nearly impossible.

1992 122m PG-13 B+

Audience: adolescents to adults
Content: language, violence
Director: Phil Alden Robinson
Lead Cast: Robert Redford, Sidney Poitier, Dan Aykroyd
Topics: ethics, heroism

SON OF THE MORNING STAR

This is a moving account of General Custer's "last stand" against the Indians in the American West after the Civil War. Narrated by women on either side of the battle, the film turns the story into a compelling account of an ambitious soldier who recklessly challenged a desperate but proud Indian leader. Adapted from the book by Evan S. Connell.

The darkness of ambition.

1991 183m PG-13 TVM A-

Audience: mature teens to adults
Content: graphic violence, adult themes
Director: Mike Robe
Lead Cast: Gary Cole, Rosana Arquette, Terry O'Quinn
Topics: death, heroism, prejudice, war

STALIN

Duvall gives a stirring performance in this docudrama about the cruel Russian leader who takes power and rules through violence and intimidation. Although a bit difficult to follow at times, the drama captures Stalin's cold, calculating character, including his troubled relationships with family. A disturbing film that says as much about human nature as about the Bolshevik Revolution.

A fine docudrama.

1992 162m NR TVM A-

Audience: adults
Content: language, violence
Director: Ivan Passer
Lead Cast: Robert Duvall, Julia Ormand
Topics: ethics, family, marriage, prejudice, war

STAND AND DELIVER

A demanding math teacher inspires a group of unmotivated Hispanic students to change the course of their lives. His unorthodox teaching style and dedication to the kids pays off as they progress from struggling with fractions to passing the Advanced Placement Test in Calculus. *Stand and Deliver* is a testimony to the power of dedication.

Inspiring true story.

1987 105m PG A-

Audience: adolescents to adults
Content: language
Director: Ramon Menendez
Lead Cast: Edward James Olmos, Lou Diamond Phillips, Rosana de Soto
Topics: adolescence, friendship, prejudice

STANLEY AND IRIS

Two factory workers help each other break out of their personal prisons to find friendship and love. The widow, Iris, has to deal with family crises on top of scraping to get by, while Stanley's options are diminishing due to illiteracy. The movie realistically portrays the stress and hardship of being caught in a life that's going nowhere, but in this warm, romantic story, "anything is possible."

A heartwarming story of friendship and love.

1990 105m PG-13 B

Audience: mature teens to adults
Content: language, mild violence, adult situations
Director: Martin Ritt
Lead Cast: Jane Fonda, Robert De Niro, Swoosie Kurtz
Topics: disability, family, friendship, romance, work

STARLIGHT HOTEL

A teenage girl runs away from home in Depression-era New Zealand after her mother dies and her father deserts her. She meets a compassionate fugitive on the road, and the two travel across the country, taking in the sights and sounds of the Depression, while avoiding authorities and facing an increasingly uncertain future.

A room with a view.

1988 93m PG A- New Zealand

Audience: teens to adults
Content: language
Director: Sam Pillsbury
Lead Cast: Peter Phelps, Greer Robson, Marshall Napier
Topics: adolescence, family, friendship

STEEL MAGNOLIAS

Five Louisiana women share their hopes and fears about life, eventually joined by a born-again Christian and her skeptical husband. As they face various joys and hardships, the group faithfully carries on as friends, mothers, wives, and workers. An honest look at faith and courage among "steel magnolias."

Celebrate the strength of the "weaker" sex.

1989 118m PG A-

Audience: adults
Content: language, adult situations and themes
Director: Herbert Ross
Lead Cast: Sally Field, Dolly Parton, Shirley MacLaine, Olympia Dukakis, Julia Roberts
Topics: death, family, friendship, marriage, parenting, work

STORY LADY, THE

A lonely widow finds a purpose reading stories on public-access TV, until she is discovered by advertising and network execs who want to transform her into a star. When things get out of hand, she needs to find some way of breaking her contract. A warm and humorous tale that gently reminds us of the joys of spending time with those we love.

The whole family can see it happily ever after.

1993 93m G TVM A

Audience: all ages
Content: nothing objectionable
Director: Larry Elikann
Lead Cast: Jessica Tandy, Stephanie Zimbalist, Lisa Jakub, Charles Durning, Richard Masur, Ed Begley Jr., Tandy Cronyn
Topics: aging, children, parenting, work

STRICTLY BALLROOM

A feisty young Australian man who dances competitively loses his partner before the big national events because he refuses to do the traditional steps. Into his life comes a Hispanic beginner, and the two decide to challenge the system with their innovative steps. Written like a contemporary fairy tale, this film's cinematic genius will steal your heart and tickle your ribs. A wonderfully innovative film.

Step into this superb movie.

1993 93m PG A Australian

Audience: adolescents to adults
Content: mild language
Director: Baz Luhrmann
Lead Cast: Paul Mercurio, Tara Morice
Topics: family, friendship, marriage, parenting, romance

SUMMER STORY, A

In turn-of-the-century England, a young attorney who doesn't believe in fate falls in love with a lower-class farm girl, and they struggle to successfully overcome the division of social class. Based on John Galsworthy's short story, "The Apple Tree," the film examines the consequences of unrequited love. Outstanding performances and cinematography.

Romantic tearjerker!

1988 94m PG-13 A- British

Audience: adults
Content: language, adult situations, nudity
Director: Piers Haggard
Lead Cast: James Wilby, Imogen Stubbs, Susannah York
Topics: marriage, romance

SWEET 15

In contemporary Los Angeles, a fourteen-year-old Hispanic girl and her family prepare for her "quince" party while her father deals with stricter government enforcement of immigrant labor laws at his business. This is a very compassionate look at the joys and sorrows among Hispanics trying to assimilate into American culture while proudly holding on to their Spanish identity.

A sweet family tale.

1990 104m NR TVM A

Audience: adolescents to adults
Content: adult themes
Director: Victoria Hochberg
Lead Cast: Karla Montana, Panchito Gomez, Tony Plana
Topics: adolescence, family, friendship, marriage, parenting, prejudice, romance

SWING KIDS

In Germany in 1939, Hitler's authority is spreading to every aspect of German life, but a determined group of teens defies the Nazis and expresses its personal freedom in the "verboten" swing music. Three teens are pulled in different directions as Hitler's power advances and they find they can no longer "swing" back and forth.

A rich story of passion and integrity.

1993 110m PG-13 A-

Audience: teens to adults
Content: language, violence, nudity
Director: Thomas Carter
Lead Cast: Robert Sean Leonard, Christian Bale, Frank Whaley, Barbara Hershey
Topics: adolescence, death, ethics, friendship, prejudice, romance, war

TAP

A gifted tap dancer returns home to New York City after several years in prison and must decide between his dance "family" and professional crime. Although predictable, the film shines because of many incredible dances and Davis's fine last screen role.

A toe-tappin' triumph.

1988 107m PG-13 A-

Audience: teens to adults
Content: language, adult situations
Director: Nick Castle
Lead Cast: Gregory Hines, Sammy Davis, Jr., Suzzanne Douglas
Topics: aging, family, marriage

THAT'S ENTERTAINMENT! III

This is another wonderful compilation of some of the best (and worst) clips from Hollywood musicals. Surviving stars (e.g., Ann Miller, Debbie Reynolds, Mickey Rooney) introduce their own performances, including split-screen outtakes. Not quite as good as the earlier MGM compilation, but still fascinating.

Memory Lane on video.

1994 111m G A-

Audience: all ages
Content: nothing objectionable
Director: Bud Friedgen, Michael J. Sheridan
Lead Cast: June Allyson, Cyd Charisse, Lena Horne, Gene Kelly, Esther Williams
Topics: romance

3 MEN AND A BABY

The lives of three swinging bachelors are drastically altered when a baby is abandoned on their doorstep, with a note naming one of the three as father. With no clue as to what they're doing, the men bungle their way and fall in love with their little "package." Though the premise of the film requires reference to sex and its consequences, and the language is somewhat overdone, the movie is hilarious. *3 Men and a Little Lady* follows.

"Bad Boys" become men.

1987 102m PG B+

Audience: adolescents to adults
Content: language, adult themes, mild violence
Director: Leonard Nimoy
Lead Cast: Tom Selleck, Steve Guttenberg, Ted Danson
Topics: children, ethics, friendship, parenting, romance, work

3 MEN AND A LITTLE LADY

Mary, the baby of *3 Men and a Baby*, is now an adorable five-year-old who lives with her mom and three "dads" until mom accepts a marriage proposal and takes Mary with her to England. If frequent references to sex can be overlooked, the story is a charming, hilarious romp, as the three men try to prevent the breakup of their "family." Not appropriate for all kids.

Rollicking good time!

1990 103m PG B

Audience: adolescents to adults
Content: mild language, adult themes
Director: Emile Ardolino
Lead Cast: Tom Selleck, Steve Guttenberg, Ted Danson, Nancy Travis, Robin Weisman
Topics: children, family, friendship, marriage, parenting, romance

THREE MUSKETEERS, THE

A young man's desire to join the musketeers leads him into adventure and political intrigue with the "three musketeers" as they fight to save King Louis XIII and France from the plotting of evil Cardinal Richelieu. Rollicking adventure for older kids and families, with a bit of history thrown in!

All for fun and fun for all!

1993 100m PG A-

Audience: adolescents to adults
Content: violence, adult themes
Director: Stephen Herek
Lead Cast: Charlie Sheen, Kiefer Sutherland, Chris O'Donnell, Oliver Platt, Rebecca DeMornay
Topics: friendship, heroism, romance

THUMBELINA

Tiny Thumbelina is kidnapped from her home by a Latin mother toad to sing in their band and marry her son—and that's only the first of her adventures as she tries to return home to be reunited with her fairy prince. A well-animated, delightfully updated version of the classic tale, with a great "cast."

Follow your heart!

1994 95m G B+ Animated

Audience: all ages
Content: nothing objectionable
Director: Don Bluth, Gary Goldman
Lead Cast: (voices) Jodi Benson, Gary Imhoff, Gino Conforti, Carol Channing, Charo, Barbara Cook, Gilbert Gottfried, John Hurt
Topics: friendship, heroism, marriage, romance

TIME TO REMEMBER, A

This is a highly sentimental story of a young Italian boy who achieves his dream of becoming an accomplished opera singer, thanks largely to the encouragement of his tenderhearted grandmother and a supportive parish priest. The child must cope with his father's disapproval as well as with considerable teasing from peers. A heartwarming story of faith and determination set at Christmastime.

On the importance of faith and family.

1986 68m G A-

Audience: all ages
Content: nothing objectionable
Director: Thomas Travers
Lead Cast: Donald O'Connor, Ruben Gomez, Morganna King
Topics: adolescence, family, friendship, parenting, religion, work

TINY TOON ADVENTURES— How I Spent My Vacation

Based on the TV series, this feature-length animated tale updates the old Looney Tunes with pint-sized versions of the well-known Warner Brothers characters. Among the summer adventures are a river raft ride, a drive-through animal safari, and a theme park.

Animated "loonacy."

1992 78m NR A- Animated

Audience: all ages
Content: mild violence
Director: Steven Spielberg
Lead Cast: (voices) Charlie Adler, Tress MacNeille, Joe Alaskey
Topics: children, family, parenting

TOBY MCTEAGUE

A young man in the Canadian North overcomes the death of his mother, falls in love, and wins a major dogsled race. Meanwhile, he and his father learn to love and respect each other. Predictable family fare made more interesting by spectacular scenery and dogsledding details.

A Canadian family flick—eh?

1986 93m PG A- Canadian

Audience: all ages
Content: language
Director: Jean-Claude Lord
Lead Cast: Wannick Bisson, Winston Rekert, Timothy Webber
Topics: adolescence, death, family, friendship, parenting, romance

TO DANCE WITH THE WHITE DOG

A lonely widower discovers a unique bond with a beautiful white dog who enters his life after his wife's death. The chemistry between Cronyn and Tandy has never been sweeter than in this touching love story about the mystery of enduring love. Based on the book by Terry Kay.

Let it move you.

1993 98m PG TVM A+

Audience: adolescents to adults
Content: nothing objectionable
Director: Glenn Jordan
Lead Cast: Hume Cronyn, Jessica Tandy
Topics: aging, death, family, romance

TOM AND JERRY: THE MOVIE

The old cartoon characters come alive (with voices) once again as the cat and mouse briefly stop squabbling to help a nearly orphaned girl find her father. Longtime fans of the duo might be disappointed, but this animated musical has its own charm and wit.

A cat-and-mouse flick.

1993 85m G B+ Animated

Audience: all ages
Content: violence
Director: Phil Roman
Cast: (voices) Richard Kiel, Dana Hill, Charlotte Rae
Topics: family, friendship

TO SLEEP WITH ANGER

This subtle but fascinating film looks at the impact of one devilish relative on the rest of a black family when he arrives unexpectedly. He plays to various family members' weaknesses, creating conflict and emotional turmoil. Although the story moves slowly, the wonderfully ironic ending is worth the wait.

A fine character study.

1990 101m PG B+

Audience: mature teens to adults
Content: adult situations
Director: Charles Burnett
Lead Cast: Danny Glover, Paul Butler, Mary Alice
Topics: aging, children, family, marriage, parenting, work

TREASURE ISLAND

In this excellent adaptation of the story by Robert Louis Stevenson, young Jim sets sail for Treasure Island in hopes of recovering priceless buried treasures. The ship is commanded by British soldiers, but the crew is a gang of pirates intent on mutiny. Most of the action takes place on the island, where Jim and the Brits battle Long John's band of cutthroat treasure hunters.

Aye, matey!

1990 131m NR TVM A-

Audience: teens to adults
Content: violence
Director: Fraser Heston
Lead Cast: Charlton Heston, Christian Bale, Julian Glover
Topics: adolescence, heroism

TUCKER: THE MAN AND HIS DREAMS

Francis Ford Coppola's tribute to the American dream is wonderfully expressed in this thoroughly enjoyable look at the irrepressible Preston Tucker, who created the "car of the future" in the months immediately after WW II. Fighting the "big-three" automakers, politicians, and corporate executives, Tucker championed many of the automotive innovations that later became standard.

An auto "tour de force."

1988 106m PG A

Audience: adolescents to adults
Content: language
Director: Francis Ford Coppola
Lead Cast: Jeff Bridges, Joan Allen, Martin Landau
Topics: ethics, family, heroism, parenting

TURNER AND HOOCH

A perfectionistic young police investigator in a sleepy California coastal town tries to solve a murder with the assistance of the deceased's slobbery canine. Along the way, he befriends the local vet, who teaches him about more than dogs. Pure comedy with a few barks of suspense and romance.

Humorous cinematic doggerel.

1989 96m PG A

Audience: all ages
Content: language, adult situations, violence
Director: Roger Spottiswoode
Lead Cast: Tom Hanks, Mare Winningham, Craig T. Nelson
Topics: romance

UNREMARKABLE LIFE, AN

The comfortable routine of a pair of aging sisters is disrupted when one meets a charming widower. While the lucky sister experiences love for the first time, the other sister's security is threatened, putting strain on relationships. Fine performances turn this simple story into a moving, bittersweet tale.

A surprising portrait of life's possibilities.

1989 97m PG B

Audience: adults
Content: adult themes
Director: Amin Q. Chaudhri
Lead Cast: Patricia Neal, Shelley Winters
Topics: aging, family, friendship, prejudice, romance

WAIT UNTIL SPRING, BANDINI

A twelve-year-old boy must step out of his childhood fantasies to pull his estranged parents back together. Frequent trips to confession help him make sense out of his imperfect world, preparing him to lead his parents to their own pride so they might eventually recognize their love for each other.

A film for all seasons.

1991 102m PG B Belgian/Italian/French

Audience: adolescents to adults
Content: adult themes, language
Director: Dominique Deruddere
Lead Cast: Joe Mantegna, Ornella Muti, Faye Dunaway
Topics: adolescence, ethics, family, marriage, religion, romance, work

WALTZ THROUGH THE HILLS, A

A boy and his younger sister are suddenly orphaned and decide to make the dangerous journey across Australia to Perth rather than being sent to an orphanage. Along the way they find unexpected help from an Aborigine. This is a story of love, determination, hope, and trust. WonderWorks.

Dance to this delightful adventure.

1988 116m NR TVM A- Australian/Canadian

Audience: adolescents to adults
Content: mild language
Director: Frank Arnold
Lead Cast: Tina Kemp, Andre Jansen, Ernie Dingo, Dan O'Herlihy
Topics: family, friendship, heroism, nature

WHALES OF AUGUST, THE

Two elderly sisters spar as they have for years in their summer retreat on an island off the Maine coast. This time, however, they realize that it might be their last summer together at the retreat. Just as the whales no longer come, they, too, may be forced to leave their beloved place. A warm glimpse of the passage into life's final stage on earth.

A rare catch!

1987 91m NR A +

Audience: teens to adults
Content: mild language
Director: Lindsay Anderson
Lead Cast: Bette Davis, Lillian Gish, Vincent Price
Topics: aging, disability, family, friendship

WHAT'S EATING GILBERT GRAPE

Gilbert has barely managed to hold together his oddly functional family, which includes his 500-pound mother and his seventeen-year-old retarded brother. Then a young woman is stranded when her camper breaks down in his small town, and he sees that life could be different. A warm film of commitment and love. DiCaprio was nominated for an Oscar for his convincing portrayal of the retarded brother.

A unique morsel.

1993 117m PG-13 A-

Audience: mature teens to adults
Content: mild violence, adult themes, language
Director: Lasse Hallstrom
Lead Cast: Johnny Depp, Juliette Lewis, Leonardo DiCaprio, Mary Steenburgen, Darlene Cates
Topics: death, disability, family, prejudice, romance

WHEN THE WHALES CAME

On a small British isle on the eve of WW I, two young children befriend a mysterious outcast who was the sole survivor of a "curse" that destroyed a neighboring island and now appears to be coming to their own home. Stunning photography and marvelous performances bring the island community to life. Based on Michael Morpurgo's story.

A wonderful catch.

1990 100M PG A-

Audience: adolescents to adults
Content: mildly frightening scenes
Director: Clive Rees
Lead Cast: Helen Mirren, Paul Scofield
Topics: adolescence, friendship, heroism, family, marriage, parenting

WHERE ANGELS FEAR TO TREAD

A recently widowed woman from the British upper class during the turn of the century falls in love with a free-spirited young Italian while on vacation. The resulting marriage produces both a child and considerable family embarrassment in England. As in other films based on E. M. Forster's novels, this one explores love and commitment in the context of an inflexible and repressive society.

For lovers of English literature.

1991 110m PG British

Audience: adults
Content: adult situations
Director: Charles Sturridge
Lead Cast: Judy Davis, Helena Bonham Carter, Rupert Graves
Topics: children, family, marriage, parenting, romance

WHERE THE RED FERN GROWS—PART TWO

An embittered young man returns home from WW II missing a leg and a sense of purpose, and it's up to Grandpa to reawaken faith and life in him. This is a tender film of renewal and trust in God. A life-affirming portrait of family love and support, well worth watching.

Visually and spiritually enlivening.

1992 92m G B

Audience: all ages
Content: language
Director: Jim McCullough
Lead Cast: Wilford Brimley, Doug McKeon, Chad McQueen
Topics: disability, ethics, family, friendship, religion, war

WHIPPING BOY, THE

A spoiled young prince in 18th-century "Brattenburg" flees the castle with his rat-chasing "whipping boy" in hopes of saving the latter's innocent sister from prison. Along the way they meet some real characters of the road and city. An excellent family film based on the Newberry novella by Sid Fleischman.

Classic Disney family fare.

1994 99m NR TVM A-

Audience: school-age to adults
Content: nothing objectionable
Director: Syd Macartney
Lead Cast: Truan Munro, George C. Scott, Kevin Conway, Nic Knight
Topics: children, friendship, parenting

WHITE FANG

A San Francisco lad bravely travels to the Alaskan wilderness to find his dead father's gold mine. He battles harsh conditions, wild animals, and mean prospectors. Eventually he adopts a wild wolf injured in an illegal dog fight. A terrific film that captures the savagery of the early Northwest and the beauty of the land. Based on Jack London's novel.

A natural!

1991 107m PG A-

Audience: adolescents to adults
Content: intense dramatic scenes
Director: Randal Kleiser
Lead Cast: Klaus Maria Brandauer, Ethan Hawke, Seymour Cassel
Topics: adolescence, nature

WHITE WOLVES

A backpacking trip turns into a wilderness survival experience for five teens when their guide is critically injured. They must each discover and use their unique gifts, put aside distrust, jealousy, and prejudice, and work together to save the life of their guide as well as to find their way out of the wilderness.

A pack of adventure!

1993 82m A-

Audience: teens to adults
Content: mild violence, intense dramatic scenes
Director: Catherine Cyran
Lead Cast: Matt McCoy, Marc Riffon, David Moscow, Ami Dolenz, Amy O'Neil, Mark Paul Gosselaar
Topics: friendship, heroism, nature, prejudice

WILDFLOWER

A young girl and her teenage brother discover a hearing-impaired, epileptic girl locked in a shed. They risk their lives to help free her from her abusive stepfather. This sensitive film deals gently with handicaps, coming-of-age, and peer pressure. It's a heartwarming story of courage and love.

A poignant, moving story.

1991 100m NR TVM A

Audience: adolescents to adults
Content: mild violence, language, intense dramatic scenes
Director: Diane Keaton
Lead Cast: Patricia Arquette, Beau Bridges, Susan Blakely
Topics: adolescence, disability, family, friendship, prejudice, romance

WILD HEARTS CAN'T BE BROKEN

A rebellious teenage girl runs away from a foster home to join a traveling show, diving on horseback from a 40-foot tower. Naively announcing, "I can do anything," she discovers the work and sacrifice necessary to live up to that statement and to achieve her dream. Based on fact, this is an incredible story of bravery and determination.

Inspiring!

1991 90m G A

Audience: school-age to adults
Content: mild violence
Director: Steve Miner
Lead Cast: Cliff Robertson, Gabrielle Anwar, Michael Schoeffling
Topics: adolescence, friendship, heroism, romance

THE BEST
CHILDREN'S VIDEO
SERIES

ADVENTURES IN ODYSSEY

Based on Focus on the Family's radio show of the same name, this video series brings the popular characters "to life" with classic animation. Each episode is filled with adventure and fantasy, while teaching a valuable lesson from the Bible. Geared for a slightly younger audience than the radio series, older preschoolers may like these, too. Titles include "The Knight Travellers," "A Fine Feathered Frenzy," and "Shadow of a Doubt."

Approx. 30m each B +
Audience: school-age and adolescents

AMERICAN SHORT STORIES COLLECTION

This series, based on various short stories by famous American writers, dramatically portrays the struggles of growing up, of being different, of finding an identity. Deep conversation starters for the family or groups. Titles include "D.P.," produced by Barry Levinson and based on the story by Kurt Vonnegut, "Almos' A Man," and "The Tell-Tale Heart" by Edgar Allen Poe. Hosted by Henry Fonda.

Various lengths, less than an hour A-
Audience: teens to adults

BABY-SITTERS CLUB, THE

This wholesome, fun-loving group of girls is every parent's dream. They juggle school, friends, responsibility—and adventure—and learn important lessons about life in the process. These entertaining live-action episodes faithfully re-create the characters and stories from the popular Baby-Sitters Club books by Ann Martin. Titles include "Dawn and the Haunted House," "Stacey's Big Break," and "Mary Anne and the Brunettes."

Approx. 30m each B +
Audience: school-age and adolescents

BUTTERCREAM GANG, THE

The ButterCream Gang was started decades ago by a group of boys who helped widows churn their milk into butter, and continues as a fun-loving gang that likes to help others. A little unrealistic, the series has worthwhile values and goals. Available only through Feature Films for Families (1-800-347-2833). Titles include "The ButterCream Gang" and "The ButterCream Gang in Secret of Treasure Mountain."

Feature-length B
Audience: school-age and adolescents

CHILDREN'S CIRCLE

A cornucopia of picture books set to video for the young child. Any child who's ever looked at a picture book can find a favorite in this series begun in the 1950s. The founding purpose was "to promote literacy by leading children back to good books and . . . to become readers." Titles include *The Emperor's New Clothes, Madeline's Rescue, The Maurice Sendak Library*, and *Happy Birthday Moon*.

Various lengths and quality B
Audience: preschool and early school-age

FAIRIE TALE THEATRE

Beloved fairy tales are brought to life by some of the finest actors (not usually associated with children's stories!) that producer Shelley Duvall could assemble. Creatively updated, with delightful attention to detail. Even adolescents will be enchanted. Titles include "Thumbelina," "The Dancing Princesses," and "Beauty and the Beast."

Approx. 45-60m each
Audience: preschool to adolescents

LAST CHANCE DETECTIVES, THE

A superb series by Focus on the Family and Tyndale House Publishers that centers on a close-knit group of four kids who begin a detective agency in an abandoned plane in the Western desert. Stunning cinematography, believable characters, and a great story provide a vehicle for biblical values.

58m each A
Audience: adolescents to adults

McGEE AND ME!

Adolescent Nicholas and his animated friend, McGee, face various trials in Nick's life in this award-winning series from Tyndale House Publishers and Focus on the Family. Biblical values are applied to everyday life as realistic answers to problems. Some of the thirteen titles include "The Big Lie," "Twister and Shout," and "Beauty in the Least."

30m each A-
Audience: school-age to adolescents

QUIGLEY'S VILLAGE

In the tradition of *Sesame Street*, Mr. Quigley shares his "village" with several other humans and a delightful bunch of puppets. Created by Christian parents to teach biblical values. Titles include "Bubba and the Big Berry," "Belly Ache," "Spike and the Terrible Tripped-Up Tapped Dance," and "Shake Ups and Showdowns."

Approx. 30m each B
Audience: preschool

RABBIT EARS PRODUCTIONS

Four different collections of stories are included in Rabbit Ears Productions—Storybook Classics, We All Have Tales (stories from around the world), American Heroes and Legends, and The Greatest Stories Ever Told (stories from the Bible). Each story is a unique blend of music, narration, and illustration.

Approx. 30m each A-
Audience: preschool and school-age

READING RAINBOW

As the song says, "you can go anywhere" in a book—or a video! Introduced by LeVar Burton, each video teaches some interesting fact that relates to the story in a way that kids will enjoy. Intended to draw kids into the fascinating world of reading.

Approx. 30m each B +
Audience: school-age

SECRET ADVENTURES

"Drea" happens to be a baby-sitter, but this isn't a *Baby-Sitters Club* clone. Secret Adventures combines live action with excellent animation to creatively weave a story around the everyday dilemmas of trying to grow up with Christian principles in a challenging world. Titles include "Spin," "Snap," and "Smash."

Approx. 30m each A-
Audience: school-age to adolescents

SHELLEY DUVALL'S BEDTIME STORIES

Shelley Duvall introduces some favorite stories from her collection. The narration by well-known actors is so warm and inviting it's like cuddling up on Grandpa's lap. Titles include "Elizabeth and Larry/Bill and Pete" and "Little Toot and the Loch Ness Monster/Choo Choo."

Approx. 25m each B
Audience: preschool and early school-age

SHELLEY DUVALL'S TALL TALES AND LEGENDS

Humorous updated versions of six favorite stories of the American West, with star-studded casts. Duvall's commitment to quality is obvious. Titles include "Annie Oakley," "Johnny Appleseed," and "Darlin' Clementine."

Approx. 50m each A-
Audience: school-age to adolescents

TALES FROM AVONLEA

After *Anne of Green Gables* and *Anne of Avonlea* (reviewed earlier), the saga continues with the *Tales From Avonlea* series based on the stories and characters in Lucy Maude Montgomery's books. A Parents' Choice Award winner, this series glows with love. Titles include "The Journey Begins" and "The Gift of Friendship."

Approx. 50m each story (2 per video) A
Audience: school-age to teens

TIMELESS TALES FROM HALLMARK

A gentler telling of many of the favorite fairy tales, with some of the scarier parts softened, and in some cases a new twist to the story. Produced with quality and taste by Hanna-Barbera. Titles include "Rapunzel" and "The Elves and Shoemaker."

Approx. 30m each B
Audience: preschool and early school-age

WALT DISNEY MINI-CLASSICS

Disney's vaults are full of wonderful short films that have been favorites for years, but tend to be overshadowed by their lavish animated features. Among them are the *Winnie-the-Pooh* series, *The Reluctant Dragon*, and *Peter and the Wolf*.

Varying times A
Audience: preschool and school-age

WONDERWORKS

Originally produced for TV by PBS, the WonderWorks series stands for excellence in family video. All deal sensitively with issues facing children and families in an engrossing drama. Many are based on classic short stories. (Some feature-length reviewed previously.) Titles include "You Must Remember This," "The Lone Star Kid," "Miracle at Moreaux," and "Bridge to Teribithia."

Most under 60m A
Audience: adolescents to adults

CLASSIC
VIDEOS

ABE LINCOLN IN ILLINOIS

Undoubtedly the best drama about honest Abe, but for some strange reason largely ignored.

1939 110m NR A
Audience: all ages
Lead Cast: Raymond Massey, Gene Lockhart

ADVENTURES OF ROBIN HOOD, THE

Hold your hats; this is the ultimate Robin Hood movie yarn, as swashbuckling as you'll ever see.

1938 106m NR A+
Audience: adolescents to adults
Lead Cast: Errol Flynn, Olivia de Havilland

ADVENTURES OF TOM SAWYER, THE

Tom has never been better portrayed on the screen, with wonderful music and a real attempt to capture Twain's character.

1938 91m NR A
Audience: all ages
Lead Cast: Tommy Kelly, Walter Brennan

AFRICAN QUEEN, THE

A tough steamboat captain and a missionary woman team up in Africa to fight the Germans—as well as each other. Directed by John Huston.

1951 105m NR A
Audience: teens to adults
Lead Cast: Humphrey Bogart, Katharine Hepburn

ALL QUIET ON THE WESTERN FRONT

German youths learn of the ravages of war in this powerful adaptation of the pacifistic novel by Erich Maria Remarque.

1930 130m NR A+
Audience: adults
Lead Cast: Lew Ayers, Louis Wolheim, John Wray, Slim Summerville

AMERICAN IN PARIS, AN

This film has it all—romance, character, and absolutely fabulous music and dance, including the longest number ever filmed.

1951 113m NR A+
Audience: adolescents to adults
Lead Cast: Gene Kelly, Leslie Caron

ANIMAL CRACKERS

The Marx Brothers meet "high culture" in a luxurious estate, and American culture will never be the same again.

1930 96m NR A
Audience: adolescents to adults
Lead Cast: Groucho, Chico, Harpo, Zeppo Marx

ANNIE

A wonderful version of the Broadway play, made lavishly with a big film budget. Great family fare.

1982 126m PG A
Audience: school-age to adults
Lead Cast: Albert Finney, Carol Burnett, Aileen Quinn, Bernadette Peters

APARTMENT, THE

A low-level company man tries to climb the corporate ladder by loaning his apartment to executives for trysts until conscience and love intervene.

1960 124m NR A-
Audience: adults
Lead Cast: Jack Lemmon, Shirley MacLaine, Fred MacMurray

AROUND THE WORLD IN 80 DAYS

A real cinematic blockbuster about an unflappable Brit and his sweet valet who try to circle the globe and win a wager. Based on the Jules Verne novel and loaded with cameo appearances.

1956 176m G A
Audience: all ages
Lead Cast: David Niven, Shirley MacLaine, Marlene Dietrich

ARSENIC AND OLD LACE

Frank Capra's production of Joseph Kesselring's play about two sweet spinsters who murder unsuspecting bachelors with elderberry wine laced with arsenic. Thoroughly madcap and wonderfully funny—one of the best comedies of all time.

1944 156m NR A +
Audience: adults
Lead Cast: Cary Grant, Pricilla Lane, Raymond Massey

AUTOBIOGRAPHY OF MISS JANE PITTMAN

A moving portrait of American blacks as seen through the eyes of a former slave who lives through the Civil War and eventually becomes part of the civil rights movement during the 1960s. One of the best television movies ever made.

1974 110m NR TVM A +
Audience: adolescents to adults
Lead Cast: Cicely Tyson, Thalmus Rasulala, Richard Dysart

BAMBI

The little deer comes to life in this incredible Disney animated tale that captures the hearts of all generations.

1942 68m NR A+ Animated
Audience: all ages
Lead Cast: (voices) Bobby Stewart, Peter Behn, Stan Alexander

BANG THE DRUM SLOWLY

The moving tale of a major-league baseball player who tries to make it through one more season while suffering with Hodgkins disease. Terrific performances based on the novel by Mark Harris.

1973 97m PG A
Audience: teens to adults
Lead Cast: Robert De Niro, Michael Moriarty, Vincent Gardenia

BECKET

A fine screen version of Jean Anouilh's play about the Archbishop of Canterbury who battles with Henry II of England over church policies and church-state relations. Superb performances from a tremendous cast.

1964 146m NR A
Audience: teens to adults
Lead Cast: Richard Burton, Peter O'Toole, John Gielgud

BELLS OF ST. MARY'S, THE

A determined sister superior and a mild-mannered priest match wits over how to run a parish school in this sequel to the popular *Going My Way*. Won eight Oscar nominations.

1945 125m NR A
Audience: adolescents to adults
Lead Cast: Ingrid Bergman, Bing Crosby, Henry Travers

BEN-HUR

This epic film about Jewish prince Ben-Hur during the time of Christ is hard to beat even today—especially the exciting chariot race. Directed by William Wyler.

1959 217m NR A
Audience: adolescents to adults
Lead Cast: Charlton Heston, Jack Hawkins, Stephen Boyd

BENJI

The best-known movie dog saves two children from kidnappers and falls in love. Cleverly told tale from the point of view of the lovable canine.

1973 86m G A-
Audience: all ages
Lead Cast: Peter Breck, Deborah Walley, Patsy Garrett

BEST YEARS OF OUR LIVES, THE

A winner of eight Academy Awards, this movie struck home with the post-WW II audience by depicting three vets trying to adjust to life back in the U.S. Directed by William Wyler.

1946 170m NR A +
Audience: adults
Lead Cast: Fredric March, Harold Russell, Myrna Loy, Dana Andrews

BIRTH OF A NATION, THE

D. W. Griffith's cinematic epic pitted the Ku Klux Klan against newly enfranchised Southern blacks after the Civil War. Although arguably racist, this was the first real American movie, and it captured the look of the era.

1915 175m NR A
Audience: teens to adults
Lead Cast: Lillian Gish, Henry B. Walthall, Mae Marsh

BISHOP'S WIFE, THE

An angel comes to earth to help a bishop who is too con-
sumed by work to love his own wife and daughter. An
unrealistic premise, but wonderfully told with the right dashes
of sentimentality.

1947 109m NR A
Audience: adolescents to adults
Lead Cast: Cary Grant, Loretta Young, David Niven

BITE THE BULLET

A western epic based on a true story about various partici-
pants of a 600-mile horse race in 1908 who come to respect
each other while battling the elements and rugged terrain. Tremendous performances.

1975 130m PG A
Audience: adolescents to adults
Lead Cast: Gene Hackman, James Coburn, Candice Bergen

BITTER HARVEST

A frenzied American dairy farmer battles governmental
bureaucracy as he tries to figure out what is mysteriously killing
his animals. Based on an actual situation.

1981 97m NR A- TVM
Audience: adolescents to adults
Lead Cast: Ron Howard, Art Carney, Tarah Nutter

BLACK STALLION, THE

A cinematic triumph based on the book about a young boy
who survives a shipwreck with a wild Arabian stallion and
befriends him on an island before rescue. (The shipwreck scene
at the beginning is far too frightening for young children.)

1979 120m G A
Audience: adolescents to adults
Lead Cast: Kelly Reno, Mickey Rooney

BORN FREE

A fine family film, with an award-winning score, about a lioness raised as a pet in Kenya.

1966 96m NR A British
Audience: all ages
Lead Cast: Virginia McKenna, Bill Travers, Geoffrey Keen, Peter Lukoye

BREAKER MORANT

Three Australian soldiers are put on trial as scapegoats for war crimes committed by British allies during the Boer War in South Africa at the turn of the century.

1979 107m PG A Australian
Audience: teens to adults
Lead Cast: Edward Woodward, Jack Thompson, John Waters, Bryan Brown

BRIAN'S SONG

A dramatization of the relationship between Chicago Bears' legend Gale Sayers and teammate Brian Piccolo, who died of cancer. A real tearjerker.

1970 73m G TVM A
Audience: all ages
Lead Cast: James Caan, Billy Dee Williams, Jack Warden

BRIDGE ON THE RIVER KWAI

Perhaps the ultimate war movie about a British colonel and his Japanese captor who battle psychologically over the building of a rail bridge by prisoners. Directed by David Lean.

1957 161m NR A+ British
Audience: adolescents to adults
Lead Cast: William Holden, Alec Guinness, Jack Hawkins

BRINGING UP BABY

One of the greatest screwball comedies of all time, based on the tale of a shy professor who searches for one bone to complete his dinosaur skeleton and meets a dog and a woman along the way.

1938 100m NR A
Audience: adolescents to adults
Lead Cast: Katharine Hepburn, Cary Grant

CASABLANCA

Oscar for best picture deservedly went to this remarkable film about a "gin-joint" operator in Nazi-occupied Morocco whose old flame arrives, creating all kinds of political intrigue and romantic possibilities. Probably the best-known American film, and certainly the most quoted.

1942 101m NR A
Audience: adults
Lead Cast: Humphrey Bogart, Ingrid Bergman, Paul Henreid

CHARIOTS OF FIRE

This sleeper about two runners in the 1924 Olympics in Paris surprised just about everyone with awards and popular acclaim. A must-see.

1981 120m PG A British
Audience: all ages
Lead Cast: Ben Cross, Ian Charleson

CHARLOTTE'S WEB

A clever spider saves a small pig from slaughter by communicating nonverbally with the superstitious farmer. Based on E. B. White's well-known children's tale, with adequate animation and fine music.

1972 93m G A Animated
Audience: all ages
Lead Cast: (voices) Debbie Reynolds, Agnes Moorehead, Paul Lynde

CHARLY

A retarded man becomes brilliant and falls in love in this outstanding production based on the novel *Flowers for Algernon*. Stock up on hankies.

1968 102m NR A
Audience: all ages
Lead Cast: Cliff Robertson, Claire Bloom

CHOSEN, THE

Two Jewish Brooklynites, one conservative and the other moderate, become friends across the cultural divide. Based on Chaim Potok's book.

1981 106m PG A-
Audience: all ages
Lead Cast: Rod Steiger, Robby Benson, Barry Miller

CHRISTMAS CAROL, A

This older version of Dickens's classic tale survives as a moving tribute to the spirit of the original story.

1951 85m NR A
Audience: adolescents to adults
Lead Cast: Alastair Sim, Kathleen Harrison, Jack Warner

CHRISTMAS STORY, A

A charming comedy in which a young boy is obsessed in 1940s America with getting a Red Ryder BB gun for Christmas, in spite of all the adults (including Santa) who warn him, "You'll shoot your eye out."

1983 93m PG A
Audience: all ages
Lead Cast: Jean Shepherd (narrator), Peter Billingsley, Melinda Dillon, Darren McGavin

CINDERELLA

Disney's classic animated version of the story combines animation, music, and (of course) singing animals.

1950 75m NR A- Animated
Audience: all ages
Lead Cast: (voices) Ilene Woods, William Phipps,
Eleanor Audley

CITIZEN KANE

A lonely publishing mogul builds a lifetime of monuments to himself, and in the process fulfills his increasingly meaningless dreams. Considered by many the best American film ever made. Directed by Orson Welles.

1941 120m NR A+
Audience: teens to adults
Lead Cast: Orson Welles, Joseph Cotten

CITY LIGHTS

In Charlie Chaplin's last silent film, the Little Tramp falls in love with a blind flower seller and tries to secure the funds to pay for her eye surgery. Moving and very funny, this silent classic was one of Chaplin's greatest achievements.

1931 86m G A+
Audience: all ages
Lead Cast: Charlie Chaplin, Virginia Cherrill

COLOR PURPLE, THE

A poor black girl survives years of abuse and intimidation in America during the first half of the 20th century to emerge as a strong, self-confident woman.

1985 152m PG-13 A
Audience: adults
Lead Cast: Danny Glover, Whoopi Goldberg, Oprah Winfrey

COURT JESTER, THE

A circus clown posing as the court jester and a band of outlaws join forces to oust a nasty king. A tremendously entertaining comedy with plenty of music and shuffle.

1956 100m NR A
Audience: all ages
Lead Cast: Danny Kaye, Glynis Johns, Basil Rathbone

C. S. LEWIS THROUGH THE SHADOWLANDS

British writer-professor Lewis has his faith challenged when he marries an American divorcée whom he meets through correspondence, only to find her health deteriorating.

1985 73m NR A-
Audience: teens to adults
Lead Cast: Joss Ackland, Claire Bloom

CYRANO DE BERGERAC

The ultimate version of the play about a tragic wit with a funny nose who desperately desires the love of a beautiful woman. Guaranteed romance.

1950 112m NR A +
Audience: adolescents to adults
Lead Cast: Jose Ferrer, Mala Powers, William Prince

DAVID COPPERFIELD

The best adaptation of Dickens's classic novel about the orphaned boy trying to mature in Victorian England.

1935 130m NR A
Audience: all ages
Lead Cast: Lionel Barrymore, W. C. Fields,
Freddie Bartholomew

DEATH OF A SALESMAN

Arthur Miller's play is performed magnificently for the small screen in this exceptional version which uses flashbacks to enhance the tragic story of lifelong salesman, Willy Lohman.

1985 135m NR TVM A
Audience: teens to adults
Lead Cast: Dustin Hoffman, John Malkovich

DIARY OF A COUNTRY PRIEST

An extremely moving account of a French priest whose first parish turns out to be a lot less—and a lot more—than he had hoped for.

1950 120m NR A+ French (subtitled)
Audience: teens to adults
Lead Cast: Claude Laydu, Jean Riveyre, Nicole Ladmiral

DIARY OF ANNE FRANK, THE

Still one of the most evocative versions of the famous true story of the Jewish girl who hid for years with her family and friends in an apartment in Nazi-occupied Amsterdam.

1959 150m NR A
Audience: adolescents to adults
Lead Cast: Millie Perkins, Joseph Schildkraut, Shelley Winters

DOCTOR ZHIVAGO

An amazing romantic epic about a young Russian intellectual and his lover who are caught in the social and cultural changes of the Bolshevik Revolution. Directed by David Lean.

1965 195m NR A
Audience: adults
Lead Cast: Omar Sharif, Julie Christie, Geraldine Chaplin

EAST OF EDEN

A marvelous adaptation of part of Steinbeck's novel, which retells the story of Cain and Abel in a more contemporary setting.

1955 105m NR A
Audience: teens to adults
Lead Cast: James Dean, Julie Harris, Richard Davalos

ELEPHANT MAN, THE

A stunning film based on the biography of John Merrick, a hideously deformed man who is saved from freak shows by a sympathetic doctor.

1980 122m PG A+
Audience: teens to adults
Lead Cast: Anthony Hopkins, John Hurt, Anne Bancroft

ELMER GANTRY

A powerful but disturbing look at religious deceit practiced by a popular evangelist in the Midwest during the 1920s. Adapted from Sinclair Lewis's novel.

1960 145m NR A
Audience: adults
Lead Cast: Burt Lancaster, Jean Simmons

E.T. THE EXTRA-TERRESTRIAL

Spielberg's tremendously popular sci fi flick is a version of the kid-and-his-dog story, with the puppy transformed into a cute little alien stranded on earth. Excellent visual effects and a terrific musical score. Too scary for some young kids.

1982 113m PG A-
Audience: school-age to adults
Lead Cast: Henry Thomas, Dee Wallace, Drew Barrymore

FANTASIA

Disney's tribute to the animal world is a marvelous combination of animated image and classical music.

1940 120m NR A Animated
Audience: all ages
Lead Cast: (narrator) Deems Taylor

FATHER OF THE BRIDE

The orginal—and best—version of the story about a middle-class American father who can't quite cope with the upcoming marriage of his cherished daughter. Wonderfully funny.

1950 92m NR A
Audience: adolescents to adults
Lead Cast: Spencer Tracy, Elizabeth Taylor

FIDDLER ON THE ROOF

The stage play is brought to cinematic life in this marvelous tale of a poor Jewish farmer who struggles with social change in a small Ukrainian village during the turn of the century. Directed by Norman Jewison.

1971 184m G A+
Audience: all ages
Lead Cast: Topol, Norma Crane, Leonard Frey

FINIAN'S RAINBOW

A leprechaun dances his way to America to reclaim the pot of gold stolen by an Irishman. An entertaining version of the Broadway musical.

1968 140m G A-
Audience: all ages
Lead Cast: Fred Astaire, Petula Clark, Keenan Wynn

FROM HERE TO ETERNITY

Eight Oscars went to this film about Army life in Hawaii before and during the Japanese attack on Pearl Harbor.

1953 112m NR A-
Audience: adults
Lead Cast: Burt Lancaster, Montgomery Clift, Deborah Kerr, Frank Sinatra

GANDHI

Mahatma Gandhi's life is chronicled as an epic, from his days as a feisty attorney to his public successes as India's political and spiritual leader, and eventually to his assassination.

1982 188m PG A + British/Indian
Audience: teens to adults
Lead Cast: Ben Kingsley, Candice Bergen, Edward Fox, John Gielgud, Trevor Howard

GOING MY WAY

A progressive young priest goes up against his more conservative superior for the benefit of the parish in this musical.

1944 126m NR A
Audience: all ages
Lead Cast: Bing Crosby, Barry Fitzgerald, Rise Stevens

GONE WITH THE WIND

The ultimate Civil War flick with plenty of battles, epic sweep, and, of course, romance. Truly an American classic.

1939 220m G A +
Audience: teens to adults
Lead Cast: Clark Gable, Vivien Leigh, Olivia de Havilland

GOOD EARTH, THE

This carefully crafted adaptation of the classic novel by Pearl S. Buck powerfully brings to life the story of a simple Chinese farm couple that faces drought, revolution, locusts, and eventual corruption by wealth. Not to be missed.

1937 135m NR A
Audience: teens to adults
Lead Cast: Paul Muni, Luise Rainer, Charley Grapewin

GRAPES OF WRATH, THE

Director John Ford marvelously captured the spirit of John Steinbeck's novel about dignity and determination among American westerners in the Dust Bowl during the Depression years. A moving story based on the award-winning novel.

1940 125m NR A
Audience: adolescents to adults
Lead Cast: Henry Fonda, Jane Darwell, John Carradine

GREATEST SHOW ON EARTH, THE

An epic of circus life, focusing on the passions and mysteries of human nature as expressed in the various circus characters. Not for everyone's taste, but a powerful film that won the Oscar for best picture.

1952 146m NR A-
Audience: teens to adults
Lead Cast: Betty Hutton, Cornel Wilde, James Stewart, Charlton Heston

GREAT EXPECTATIONS

Probably the best film based on a Charles Dickens novel, this one follows young Pip, an orphan who gets a mysterious gift and becomes a society man in England.

1946 117m NR A-
Audience: school-age to adults
Lead Cast: John Mills, Valerie Hobson, Bernard Miles

GUESS WHO'S COMING TO DINNER

A white college coed surprises her parents by bringing home a black man for dinner, creating insightful family dynamics about prejudice. The all-star cast makes this a wonderful movie. Directed by Stanley Kramer.

1967 107m NR A-
Audience: teens to adults
Lead Cast: Katharine Hepburn, Spencer Tracy, Sidney Poitier

HAMLET

Undoubtedly the best version of Shakespeare's play, although a few scenes were eliminated from the script.

1948 153m NR A British
Audience: teens to adults
Lead Cast: Laurence Olivier, Basil Sydney, Felix Aylmer

HARVEY

Stewart excels in this filmic version of the Mary Chase play about an affable drunk who believes that he has a six-foot rabbit for a friend.

1950 102m NR A-
Audience: teens to adults
Lead Cast: James Stewart, Josephine Hull

HIGH NOON

Cooper is a marshal who has to battle four hired guns without the help of cowardly town folk before he can marry his fiancée. One of the best westerns ever. Directed by Fred Zinnemann.

1952 85m NR A
Audience: adolescents to adults
Lead Cast: Gary Cooper, Grace Kelly, Lloyd Bridges

HOW THE WEST WAS WON

An epic tale of three generations of American pioneers, loaded with terrific performances, exceptional photography, and a marvelous score.

1962 154m NR A
Audience: adolescents to adults
Lead Cast: George Peppard, Debbie Reynolds, James Stewart, Henry Fonda

I NEVER SANG FOR MY FATHER

A moving film based on Robert Anderson's play about an adult son who is torn between caring for his father and marrying the woman he loves.

1970 90m PG A
Audience: adults
Lead Cast: Gene Hackman, Melvyn Douglas, Estelle Parsons

INHERIT THE WIND

The endlessly relevant battle of faith and science set in a fictionalization of the famous Scopes trial of 1925.

1960 126m NR A-
Audience: adolescents to adults
Lead Cast: Spencer Tracy, Fredric March, Florence Eldridge, Gene Kelly

IN THE HEAT OF THE NIGHT

A powerful tale of Southern life about a black man who helps solve a murder even though he is the principal suspect. Directed by Norman Jewison.

1967 107m NR A-
Audience: adults
Lead Cast: Sidney Poitier, Rod Steiger, Warren Oates

I REMEMBER MAMA

A timeless tale based on John Druten's play about a Norwegian family that emigrates to the Bay Area in the early years of the century.

1948 134m NR A-
Audience: school-age to adults
Lead Cast: Irene Dunne, Barbara Bel Geddes, Oscar Homolka

IT'S A WONDERFUL LIFE

Frank Capra's enormously popular tale about a suicidal man at Christmastime whose guardian angel takes him on a tour of the past good he's actually accomplished. A real heartwarmer.

1946 125m NR A+
Audience: all ages
Lead Cast: James Stewart, Donna Reed, Henry Travers, Lionel Barrymore

JESUS OF NAZARETH

Directed by Franco Zefferelli, this masterful biblical epic depicts the life of Christ with sensitivity and grace.

1976 371m NR A
Audience: school-age to adults.
Lead Cast: Robert Powell, Anne Bancroft, James Mason, Rod Steiger

JOURNEY OF NATTY GANN, THE

In Depression-era America, a clever teenage girl journeys bravely from Chicago to the Pacific Northwest to find her father who left her behind to get work.

1985 96m PG A
Audience: school-age to adults
Lead Cast: Meredith Salenger, John Cusack, Ray Wise

KING AND I, THE

Rodgers and Hammerstein's musical is lovingly adapted to the screen as we witness the battle of wits between an English governess and the King of Siam over raising children in the modern world.

1956 133m G A
Audience: all ages
Lead Cast: Deborah Kerr, Yul Brynner, Rita Moreno

LADY AND THE TRAMP

Disney's animated classic follows two dogs who fall in love—one a tramp and the other a spoiled pet. Terrific music and clever animation.

1955 76m G A Animated
Audience: all ages
Lead Cast: (voices) Peggy Lee (really), Larry Roberts, Barbara Luddy

LAWRENCE OF ARABIA

A marvelous, richly photographed epic about T. E. Lawrence, a British citizen who helps the Arab Bedouin battle the Turks during WW I. Winner of many awards. Directed by David Lean.

1962 205m G A +
Audience: school-age to adults
Lead Cast: Peter O'Toole, Alec Guinness, Anthony Quinn

LES MISERABLES

Victor Hugo's classic novel of forgiveness in 18th-century France is marvelously brought to cinematic life. Better than the later versions.

1935 104m NR A
Audience: adolescents to adults
Lead Cast: Fredric March, Charles Laughton

LIFE WITH FATHER

A delightful tale of family life in New York City during the 1880s, with a stern father, four sons, and a wise mother. Based on writing of Clarence Day, Jr.

1947 117m NR A-
Audience: all ages
Lead Cast: William Powell, Irene Dunne, Elizabeth Taylor

LILIES OF THE FIELD

A reluctant U.S. Army veteran gets roped into helping five East German nuns build a chapel and learn English after they flee the country.

1963 94m NR A-
Audience: adolescents to adults
Lead Cast: Sidney Poitier, Lilia Skala, Lisa Mann

LITTLE WOMEN

A true classic about four sisters growing up during the Civil War. Based on Louisa May Alcott's novel. A real tearjerker.

1933 115m NR A+
Audience: school-age to adults
Lead Cast: Katharine Hepburn, Joan Bennett

LONGEST DAY, THE

A star-studded cast and Oscar-winning special effects and cinematography capture the great, though sometimes tragic, invasion of Normandy by Allied forces during World War II.

1962 180m NR A
Audience: teens to adults
Lead Cast: John Wayne, Rod Steiger, Robert Ryan, Peter Lawford, Henry Fonda, Robert Mitchum, Richard Burton

LOST HORIZON

A romantic tearjerker about a captured British diplomat and other travelers who are taken to a mysterious place in Tibet where people live for hundreds of years. Directed by Frank Capra.

1937 130m NR A-
Audience: teens to adults
Lead Cast: Ronald Colman, Jane Wyatt

MAGIC FLUTE, THE

A wonderful version of Mozart's famous comic opera about a prince who has to save the kidnapped daughter of the queen. Staged before a live audience, in Swedish with subtitles.

1973 134m G A Swedish
Audience: all ages
Lead Cast: Josef Kostlinger, Irma Urrila

MALTESE FALCON, THE

Detective Sam Spade searches for the mysterious statuette after his partner dies. Based on Dashiell Hammett's novel.

1941 100m NR A
Audience: adolescents to adults
Lead Cast: Humphrey Bogart, Mary Astor, Sidney Greenstreet, Peter Lorre

MAN CALLED PETER, A

An inspiring dramatization of the life of Peter Marshall, a Scottish pastor who eventually became chaplain to the U.S. Senate.

1955 119m NR A-
Audience: all ages
Lead Cast: Richard Todd, Jean Peters

MANCHURIAN CANDIDATE, THE

A young Korean War veteran believes that his heroic comrade may have been brainwashed into being an assassin. A powerful thriller about psychological war in the modern world. Directed by John Frankenheimer.

1962 126m PG-13 A
Audience: adults
Lead Cast: Frank Sinatra, Laurence Harvey

MAN FOR ALL SEASONS, A

A biographical drama about the life of Sir Thomas More, a 16th-century British leader who battled with King Henry VIII over the latter's desire to divorce Catherine of Aragon so he could marry his mistress. Directed by Fred Zinnemann.

1966 120m G A British
Audience: teens to adults
Lead Cast: Paul Scofield, Robert Shaw, Orson Welles

MAN FROM SNOWY RIVER, THE

A young man must prove himself to his boss and fellow hands to overcome their scorn of "mountain men," as well as to win the love of the boss's daughter.

1982 104m PG A Australian
Audience: adolescents to adults
Lead Cast: Kirk Douglas, Tom Burlinson, Sigrid Thornton

MARTY

A shy, good-hearted bachelor falls in love but faces considerable difficulty freeing himself from both family and personal self-doubts. Earlier TV version is also excellent.

1955 90m NR A
Audience: adolescents to adults
Lead Cast: Ernest Borgnine, Betsy Blair

MARY POPPINS

A delightfully wacky tale about a magical British nanny and a dancing chimney sweep who introduce the children of a proper British businessman to fun and imagination.

1964 137m NR A
Audience: all ages
Lead Cast: Julie Andrews, Dick Van Dyke

MASS APPEAL

A popular priest from a wealthy suburban congregation reluctantly mentors an altruistic seminarian in this thought-provoking comedy based on the Broadway hit by Bill C. Davis.

1984 96m PG A-
Audience: mature teens to adults
Lead Cast: Jack Lemmon, Zeljko Ivanek, Charles Durning

MIRACLE ON 34TH STREET

When a department store in New York City hires the "real" Kris Kringle as Santa Claus, Kris has to prove his authenticity.

1947 96m NR A-
Audience: all ages
Lead Cast: Maureen O'Hara, John Payne, Edmund Gwenn, Natalie Wood

MIRACLE WORKER, THE

A terrific movie version of the Broadway play about Helen Keller's triumphal entry into human relationships through the work of her dedicated teacher. Extremely moving.

1962 105m NR A+
Audience: all ages
Lead Cast: Anne Bancroft, Patty Duke, Victor Jory

MODERN TIMES

Factory worker Chaplin goes nutty from his assembly-line job and decides to do battle with the machine world. A wildly funny film with many gags that were used repeatedly in later movies. Mostly silent.

1936 87m NR A
Audience: all ages
Lead Cast: Charlie Chaplin, Paulette Goddard

MR. SMITH GOES TO WASHINGTON

One of Frank Capra's finest films about a virtuous scout leader who becomes a U.S. senator and must fight for truth and justice against seemingly insurmountable odds.

1939 128m NR A
Audience: adolescents to adults
Lead Cast: James Stewart, Jean Arthur, Claude Rains

MUPPETS TAKE MANHATTAN, THE

Kermit the Frog, Miss Piggy, and the rest of the Muppet gang graduate from college and take their variety show to Broadway in this celebration and satire of show business.

1984 92m G A-
Audience: all ages
Lead Cast: (voices) Jim Henson, Frank Oz, Jerry Nelson

MUSIC MAN, THE

A wildly humorous, deeply affectionate, marvelously musical look at middle America, love and family, when a con artist arrives in small-town Iowa to sell musical instruments and enjoy the local ladies before skipping town.

1962 151m NR A
Audience: all ages
Lead Cast: Robert Preston, Shirley Jones, Buddy Hackett

MUTINY ON THE BOUNTY

By far the best version of the classic tale of mean Captain Bligh who savagely lords it over his crew aboard the HMS Bounty.

1935 132m NR A
Audience: teens to adults
Lead Cast: Clark Gable, Franchot Tone, Charles Laughton

NATIONAL VELVET

A truly family tale about a girl and an ex-jockey who train for England's national steeplechase competition. Probably the best of all of the girl-and-horse movies.

1945 123m G A
Audience: all ages
Lead Cast: Mickey Rooney, Elizabeth Taylor

NATURAL, THE

After a sixteen-year absence, a middle-aged man returns to professional baseball to fulfill his childhood dream of stardom, only to find that his body and memories get in the way of his dream.

1984 134m PG A-
Audience: adolescents to adults
Lead Cast: Robert Redford, Glenn Close, Robert Duvall

NEVER CRY WOLF

Writer Farley Mowat goes to the Canadian Arctic alone to study the lives of wolves, and finds out a lot about himself as well as wolves.

1983 103m PG A-
Audience: adolescents to adults
Lead Cast: Charles Martin Smith

NIGHT AT THE OPERA, A

The Marx brothers do comedic battle with the snooty world of grand opera, including patrons, directors, and audiences. Perhaps their funniest film.

1935 95m NR A
Audience: all ages
Lead Cast: Groucho, Chico, Harpo Marx

NUN'S STORY, THE

A free-spirited nun working in a Belgian mental hospital and a Congolese hospital during WW II tries to reconcile her faith with the real world. Intense tale based on Kathryn Hulme's novel.

1959 150m NR A-
Audience: adults
Lead Cast: Audrey Hepburn, Peter Finch

OLD YELLER

A fine movie version of Fred Gipson's novel about a family, a young boy, and a dog in 19th-century Texas.

1957 82m G A-
Audience: all ages
Lead Cast: Dorothy McGuire, Fess Parker

OLIVER

Dickens's *Oliver Twist* is brought to the screen in real style with big-budget musical numbers. A treat for all ages.

1968 145m G A British
Audience: all ages
Lead Cast: Mark Lester, Ron Moody, Jack Wild

101 DALMATIANS

Disney classic animated tale about a male dalmatian who arranges for his master to meet a woman with a pretty female dalmatian. Of course pups arrive soon. Comedy with a bit of scary action.

1961 77m G A Animated
Audience: all ages
Lead Cast: (voices) Rod Taylor, Betty Lou Gerson

ON THE WATERFRONT

Eight Academy Awards went to this powerful film about New York dockworkers who get deeply involved in union politics and even crime.

1954 108m NR A
Audience: adults
Lead Cast: Marlon Brando, Rod Steiger, Eva Marie Saint

OUR TOWN

A fine television version of Thornton Wilder's famous play about daily life in a small New England town at the turn of the century. Fine film version (1940) also available.

1977 120m NR A
Audience: school-age to adults
Lead Cast: Ned Beatty, Sada Thompson

PARENT TRAP, THE

Disney's puffy tale about twin sisters who conspire to reunite their divorced parents. Kids still like the zany antics. Better than the sequels.

1961 125m NR A-
Audience: all ages
Lead Cast: Hayley Mills, Maureen O'Hara, Brian Keith

PASSION OF JOAN OF ARC, THE

A remarkable silent film depicting the tragic life of the saint who refused to abide by the church's rulings.

1928 114m NR A- French
Audience: adults
Lead Cast: Maria Falconetti, Eugene Silvain

PATTON

The controversial World War II general is brilliantly portrayed by Scott in this fascinating film that won seven Oscars.

1970 169m NR A
Audience: teens to adults
Lead Cast: George C. Scott, Karl Malden, Stephen Young, Michael Strong, Frank Latimore

PICTURE OF DORIAN GRAY, THE

A young British aristocrat maintains his handsome, youthful appearance while his portrait reveals the horror of his soul, in this haunting story adapted from the work of Oscar Wilde.

1945 111m NR A-
Audience: adolescents to adults
Lead Cast: Hurd Hatfield, Donna Reed, Angela Lansbury, George Sanders

PINOCCHIO

Superb animation by Disney turns the well-known tale about a wooden puppet into a joyful story of music and fun. A few scenes might scare younger kids.

1940 86m G A Animated
Audience: all ages
Lead Cast: (voices) Dick Jones, Cliff Edwards

PLACES IN THE HEART

In Depression-era Texas, a faithful widow tries to make ends meet with the help of an unlikely farmhand and a blind war veteran.

1984 108m PG A
Audience: adolescents to adults
Lead Cast: Sally Field, Lindsay Crouse, Ed Harris, Danny Glover

POLLYANNA

A timeless version of the tale about an unflappably optimistic orphan who goes to live with her wealthy aunt in New England in the early years of the century.

1960 130m G A
Audience: all ages
Lead Cast: Hayley Mills, Jane Wyman

PRIDE OF THE YANKEES

This touching biography follows baseball's great Lou Gehrig from his first childhood interest in the game to the peak of his career, when illness struck.

1942 127m NR A
Audience: adolescents to adults
Lead Cast: Gary Cooper, Teresa Wright, Babe Ruth, Walter Brennan

QUIET MAN, THE

An Irish boxer returns to his native land to make peace with his past and to settle down with a wife who is not easy to get along with. Wonderfully photographed tale directed by John Ford.

1952 127m NR A
Audience: teens to adults
Lead Cast: John Wayne, Maureen O'Hara

RAILWAY CHILDREN

The father of three children is unfairly imprisoned in turn-of-the century Britain, and they and their mother try to survive as well as figure out how to gain his release. Based on Edith Nesbitt's novel; directed by Lionel Jeffries.

1970 103m G A-
Audience: school-age to adults
Lead Cast: Jenny Agutter, William Mervyn

REBEL WITHOUT A CAUSE

A powerful tale of troubled teenagers' search for love and acceptance—perhaps *the* movie about delinquency and the generation gap.

1955 110m NR A-
Audience: teens to adults
Lead Cast: James Dean, Natalie Wood, Sal Mineo

RED RIVER

A mean-spirited father and his son battle during an enormous cattle drive in the American West. A fine epic and one of the best westerns ever filmed. Directed by Howard Hawks.

1948 130m NR A
Audience: adolescents to adults
Lead Cast: John Wayne, Montgomery Clift, Walter Brennan

RED SHOES, THE

Perhaps the best movie about ballet, this romantic story follows an ambitious ballerina who is torn between career and love. Best picture nominee.

1948 130m NR A British
Audience: adolescents to adults
Lead Cast: Anton Walbrook, Moira Shearer

ROBIN HOOD

The classic tale is told with a new and funny twist—animated animals as all of the characters (would you believe the sheriff's sidekick is a snake?).

1973 82m NR A Animated

Audience: all ages
Lead Cast: (voices) Brian Bedford, Phil Harris, Roger Miller, Peter Ustinov

ROOTS

Alex Haley's popular television miniseries follows the history of a black family from the slave trade to the quest for freedom in America. Six tapes.

1977 540m NR TVM A

Audience: teens to adults
Lead Cast: Ed Asner, LeVar Burton, Ben Vereen, Louis Gossett, Jr.

SAY AMEN, SOMEBODY

This is an inspiring documentary, with plenty of music, about the early years of gospel music, when Thomas A. Dorsey and others adapted the blues for urban black churches.

1982 100m G A

Audience: all ages
Lead Cast: (performers) Thomas Dorsey, Willie Mae Smith, Sallie Martin, the Barrett Sisters, the O'Neal Brothers

SEARCHERS, THE

Perhaps the best western ever made, a moving tale of a Civil War veteran who searches doggedly for seven years for his niece, who was kidnapped by Indians.

1956 119m NR A+

Audience: teens to adults
Lead Cast: John Wayne, Jeffrey Hunter, Vera Miles

SECRET OF NIMH, THE

A wonderfully entertaining animated version of Robert C. O'Brien's children's book about a widowed mouse who enlists the help of other critters to save her brood.

1982 80m G A Animated
Audience: all ages
Lead Cast: (voices) Elizabeth Hartman, Derek Jacobi, Dom DeLuise

SERGEANT YORK

A religious pacifist is drafted to fight in World War II, becoming the most decorated hero of the conflict.

1941 134m NR A-
Audience: adolescents to adults
Lead Cast: Gary Cooper, Walter Brennan, Joan Leslie, George Tobias, Stanley Ridges

SHANE

A former gunfighter helps Wyoming homesteaders threatened by a ruthless land magnate. Nominated for five Academy Awards.

1953 118m NR A
Audience: teens to adults
Lead Cast: Alan Ladd, Jean Arthur, Van Heflin

SINGIN' IN THE RAIN

One of the greatest musicals made, about a silent-movie star in the 1920s who is caught in the change to sound while romancing a young actress. Terrific music and performances.

1952 103m NR A+
Audience: adolescents to adults
Lead Cast: Gene Kelly, Donald O'Connor, Jean Hagen, Debbie Reynolds

SLEEPING BEAUTY

Disney's animated version of Charles Perrault's popular story includes Tchaikovsky's ballet music and superb technical methods for the time.

1959 75m G A Animated
Audience: all ages
Lead Cast: (voices) Mary Costa, Bill Shirley, Vera Vague

SNOW WHITE AND THE SEVEN DWARFS

Snow White lives in the forest with wacky dwarfs to hide from the jealous queen. Terrific music and superb animation make this among the best Disney animated classics.

1937 82m G A Animated
Audience: all ages
Lead Cast: (voices) Adriana Caselotti, Harry Stockwell, Lucille Laverne

SOMEWHERE IN TIME

A playwright falls in love with an actress pictured in a photo from 1912, and through hypnosis travels back to be with her. A witty, sincere tale.

1980 103m PG A
Audience: adults
Lead Cast: Christopher Reeve, Jane Seymour, Christopher Plummer

SOUNDER

A black family of sharecroppers in rural Louisiana tries to survive the Depression when the father is sent to jail for stealing. Based on William Armstrong's novel.

1972 105m G A
Audience: all ages
Lead Cast: Paul Winfield, Cicely Tyson, Kevin Hooks

SOUND OF MUSIC, THE

Perhaps the best-loved movie of all time, a simple tale of the Von Trapp family that has to flee native Austria to escape the Nazis before World War II. Directed by Robert Wise.

1965 173m G A+
Audience: all ages
Lead Cast: Julie Andrews, Christopher Plummer, Eleanor Parker

STAGECOACH

A classic western in which an unlikely group of coach riders is attacked by bandits and Indians. Better than later versions. Directed by John Ford.

1939 100m NR A
Audience: adolescents to adults
Lead Cast: John Wayne, Claire Trevor, Thomas Mitchell

STAR WARS

One of the first well-made sci-fi "westerns," in which the young hero battles the evil empire of the galaxy. Humor, drama, and terrific special effects. Directed by George Lucas.

1977 120m PG A
Audience: adolescents to adults
Lead Cast: Mark Hamill, Carrie Fisher, Harrison Ford

SWISS FAMILY ROBINSON, THE

A family shipwrecks on a deserted tropical island while fleeing Napoléon. There they build a fortress against a pirate. Based on Johann Wyss's novel.

1960 125m G A-
Audience: adolescents to adults
Lead Cast: John Mills, Dorothy McGuire

TALE OF TWO CITIES, A

A deeply moving adaptation of the Dickens novel about two men who love the same girl during the French Revolution.

1935 128m NR A
Audience: adolescents to adults
Lead Cast: Ronald Colman, Elizabeth Allan, Edna May Oliver

TEN COMMANDMENTS, THE

One of the best Bible epics, about Moses leading the Jews out of Egypt. Includes the parting of the Red Sea, a remarkable special effect yet today. Directed by Cecil B. DeMille.

1956 218m G A
Audience: school-age to adults
Lead Cast: Charlton Heston, Yul Brynner, Anne Baxter

TENDER MERCIES

A down-and-out country music writer unexpectedly finds grace in the rugged land of rural Texas, thanks largely to his new wife and stepson.

1983 89m PG A +
Audience: adolescents to adults
Lead Cast: Robert Duvall, Tess Harper, Betty Buckley

TESTAMENT

A strong-willed mother and her three children in a small California town try to find hope amid the ravages of a nearby nuclear attack that casts the people into despair and anger.

1984 90m PG TVM A
Audience: adults
Lead Cast: Jane Alexander, William Devane

THAT'S ENTERTAINMENT!

A remarkable compilation of some of the best numbers from MGM musicals, from "The Broadway Melody" to "Gigi."

1974 130m G A

Audience: all ages
Lead Cast: Fred Astaire, Liza Minnelli, Frank Sinatra, Gene Kelly, Bing Crosby

THAT'S ENTERTAINMENT, PART 2

A second wonderful collection of MGM musical numbers, including scenes from "The Thin Man" and the Marx Brothers' "A Night at the Opera."

1976 131m G A

Audience: all ages
Lead Cast: Fred Astaire, Gene Kelly

THIRD MAN, THE

A writer of pulp westerns searches in Vienna after WW II for his friend. Great intrigue and fabulous performances.

1949 104m NR A- British

Audience: teens to adults
Lead Cast: Orson Welles, Joseph Cotten

TO KILL A MOCKINGBIRD

Horton Foote's superb adaptation of the powerful novel by Harper Lee about a Southern lawyer who defends an innocent black man accused of raping a white woman.

1962 129m NR A +

Audience: teens to adults
Lead Cast: Gregory Peck, Brock Peters, Phillip Alford

TOMORROW

A marvelous film version of Steinbeck's haunting tale about a poor, kindhearted Southern farmhand who raises a boy left with him by a deserted woman.

1972 102m PG A
Audience: adolescents to adults
Lead Cast: Robert Duvall, Olga Bellin, Sudie Bond

TOOTSIE

An out-of-work actor is so desperate for a job that he re-creates himself as a woman and lands a part in a popular soap opera. Ten Oscar nominations.

1982 116m PG A
Audience: teens to adults
Lead Cast: Dustin Hoffman, Jessica Lange, Teri Garr

TRIP TO BOUNTIFUL, A

A feisty elderly widow runs away from her son's and daughter's strained hospitality for one last visit to her childhood home in the country.

1985 106m PG A
Audience: adults
Lead Cast: Geraldine Page, Rebecca De Mornay, John Heard

TOUCH OF EVIL

Orson Welles's frightening tale follows the attempts by a cop to investigate a murder in a U.S.-Mexico border town where the detective is corrupt. A stark look at evil and deception.

1958 95m NR A-
Audience: adults
Lead Cast: Charlton Heston, Janet Leigh, Orson Welles

TREASURE OF THE SIERRA MADRE, THE

Three prospectors travel through Mexico in search of gold. A superb story of greed and desperation. Directed by John Huston.

1948 126m NR A
Audience: teens to adults
Lead Cast: Humphrey Bogart, Walter Huston, Tim Holt

20,000 LEAGUES UNDER THE SEA

Jules Verne's tale comes to life as Captain Nemo battles the surface world from his submarine. Wait, a scientist and a sailor are on his trail!

1954 126m G A
Audience: adolescents to adults
Lead Cast: Kirk Douglas, James Mason, Peter Lorre

WEST SIDE STORY

In New York's West Side, gang fights and racism haunt the growing love between two teens. Fabulous music, terrific performances, and a solid message just as relevant today. Directed by Robert Wise.

1961 151m NR A
Audience: adolescents to adults
Lead Cast: Natalie Wood, Richard Beymer, Russ Tamblyn, Rita Moreno

WHERE THE RED FERN GROWS

A family story about a young boy in Depression Oklahoma who finds companionship in two dogs—until tragedy strikes. Based on the book.

1974 95m G A-
Audience: school-age to adults
Lead Cast: James Whitmore, Beverly Garland, Jack Ging

WILLY WONKA AND THE CHOCOLATE FACTORY

An endearing musical based on R. Dahl's popular book about the strange manager of a chocolate factory who leads lucky contest winners on a tour of the plant.

1971 98m G A
Audience: all ages
Lead Cast: Gene Wilder, Jack Albertson

WIND IN THE WILLOWS, THE

Toad, Mole, Ratty, and Kenneth Grahame's other beloved characters come to life in this fine animated version of the classic tale.

1983 60m NR A Animated
Audience: all ages
Lead Cast: (voices) Michael Hordern, Ian Carmichael, David Jason

WIZARD OF OZ, THE

Young Dorothy and her friends must battle the Wicked Witch if Dorothy is ever to get back to Kansas from this fantasyland. Pure entertainment. Based on the book.

1939 100m NR A +
Audience: all ages
Lead Cast: Judy Garland, Margaret Hamilton, Ray Bolger, Bert Lahr, Jack Haley

WUTHERING HEIGHTS

The first and the best movie version of Emily Brontë's novel about the doomed romance between two lovers in the moors of England.

1939 104m NR A
Audience: adults
Lead Cast: Laurence Olivier, Merle Oberon, David Niven

YOU CAN'T TAKE IT WITH YOU

A wacky story based on the Hart-Kaufman play about a nutty New York family and their unusual houseguests who somehow rise above their own zaniness to see the good in it all.

1938 126m NR A
Audience: teens to adults
Lead Cast: James Stewart, Jean Arthur, Lionel Barrymore

INDEX

206